DEAR NICOLE, I LOVE YOU CHAIR

The Healing Power of Remembered Love

Jerry Bongard

authorHOUSE®

AuthorHouse™
1663 Liberty Drive
Bloomington, IN 47403
www.authorhouse.com
Phone: 1-800-839-8640

First published by AuthorHouse   5/13/2010

ISBN: 978-1-4520-1048-9 (e)
ISBN: 978-1-4520-1046-5 (sc)
ISBN: 978-1-4520-1047-2 (hc)

Library of Congress Control Number: 2010906181

Printed in the United States of America
Bloomington, Indiana

This book is printed on acid-free paper.

Dear Reader,

This book is written for my granddaughter Nicole but it is also written for you. It is meant as an invitation. As you will read in the following pages, we all need an invitation to live. You have already received many invitations from those who love you, inviting you to live. This book is another such invitation, inviting you to live with enthusiasm, to enjoy this ride on planet earth as we circle the sun together and to feel the exhilaration of the ride.

You are meant to have an abundant life, one where love conquers fear, where the courage to be yourself takes root in your heart, in your soul.

I do not believe this book has come into your hands by accident. I write with hope and with love for the world we share, and for you to live the life you are meant to live.

Jerry Bongard
May 2010

For my wife Gail, my brother Tom

And

For Anna

Acknowledgements

This is written to and for my granddaughter Nicole Frohreich, one of four amazing grandchildren.

I dedicate it to my wife Gail and to my brother Tom. Their courage and love amaze and inspire me, and I hope they know how much I love them.

Thanks to my daughters Laurie, Mary, and Julie for their encouragement and steadfast love, and to my four grandchildren: Justin, Aaron, Nicole, and Kyle for their honesty in questioning what is true and good for them. They are such a joy for me. Nicole, bless your wonderful heart for your inspiration and for the Afterword.

Julie, you also are a model of enthusiastic and joyful love. Thanks for writing the Foreword.

Kyle, thanks for the title and the story behind it.

Thanks to my sisters Cindy and Carol who gave early encouragement and who have been lifelong companions. I love them dearly, and find joy in them and in their families.

Thanks to Bill Malcomson, Floic Vane, Hal Zina Bennet, and Nancy Slind, who were supportive from the beginning.

Thanks to Joan Bissel for the story of Coyote, Fox, and Helldiver.

Anna Holzemer is an inspiration.

Thanks to our pastor, Deb Benson for her model of a good minister. If all clergy were like her, the Church would never have been in need of reform.

Dave and Karen, Allison, Harry, and Peggy are inspirations for me and for many years have been in my heart.

Thanks to my parents whose struggle with faith has motivated me to also struggle.

I love all of these people as well as the extended families of my daughters and siblings.

And thanks to the many people in my life for their lives of love, especially the memory of James P. Shannon – Priest, Bishop, Mentor, and Friend.

Jerry Bongard, May, 2010

Foreward
By Julie Bongard

I've never written a "Foreword" for a book before. At a loss for knowing where to even begin, I checked Wikipedia for some answers as to what should be included, and here's a snippet of what I found...

"Often, a foreword will tell of some interaction between the writer of the foreword and the story or the writer of the story."

The writer of this story and I have 40 years of interactions from which to pull from... he's my dad. My hero. My light and my knight in shining armor. He's my rock and my role model. The acronym WWJD for me, more often, changes to WWDD... What Would Dad Do..? He is, as I tell anyone who has not met him, as close to Jesus as anyone could come... biased? Yes. But not too far from reality. The past few years he has been working on the book, writing, pacing, thinking, writing... and I've heard much about the process as he hammered through each chapter. We ALL have heard so much about it, SO MUCH, that my mother suggested that I mention how ECSTATIC we are that it is finally finished. :) That eventful day a few months ago when he strode so proudly into the room with the widest smile ever... proclaiming the great news... "I have finished the book and it's ready for publication!" was followed just a couple of hours later, with a full cup of coffee being spilled across the computer hard drive... a collective gasp of horror for those of us nearby, not believing such ironic misfortune of Murphy's Law. Fortunately with the grace he lives by on a daily basis we all survived the coffee incident (which I find quite funny looking back) as the back up copies and computer experts saved us all the dreaded fate of reliving continued years of re-writing.

I am not only proud of my father for who he is and for this great accomplishment of completing his second book, but I am especially proud of what it stands for. Humans are raised to believe certain values and 'truths' from the moment they are born, but based on the haphazard luck of where we may have been born, these 'truths' vary from culture to culture, and from religion to religion. I was raised to think that the

Christian path was the only true path to salvation. We begin to believe whole heartedly that what we are told by our parents, our churches, our culture is our truth.

I was married once... and one thing my husband used to try to remind himself almost daily, while also reminding me...in a marriage it's important to remember "My way is not the only way, my way is not the only way..." This was often his mantra. I've come to learn that this mantra is a necessity in helping to understand other cultures and other religions as well as even our history. With hundreds of different religions, how can we tell them we, as Christians, are the only ones with the correct answers? How, even more importantly, can anybody justify hatred, murder, discrimination... to someone just because they are different from US? Thus, the THEM VS. US conflicts that are the focus of this book, and the focus of so much war and pain and suffering throughout history.

My ex husband was sure right on with his chant "my way is not the only way my way is not the only way my way is not the only way" ... sometimes a hard concept to grasp as humans we so often want to be RIGHT all the time ... but ... we need to accept the ways of those who are different from US, and love people not despite our differences, but because of them. There is one great exception however...and if I may summarize the hard work and years of writing and re-writing and revising of my father into one simple phrase of what he's trying to tell us as the readers... LOVE is -THE ONLY WAY-.

Contents

Dear Reader,   v
Acknowledgements   vii
Foreward   ix
Introduction   xiii

PART ONE: STORIES AS WISDOM

1. Stories, The Bible, and Us   3
2. Kindling the Sacred Fire   9
3. He Who Holds the Sky With Both Hands   13
4. What You See is What You Get   19
5. Remembering Who We Are   23
6. Abraham, Monotheism and the Bible   27

PART TWO: HUMAN NATURE

7. We Need to be One of Us   37
8. It Can Be a Matter of Life and Death   41
9. Us Against Them   45
10. We Are Against Them in order to be Part of Us   51
11. We Need an Invitation to Live   57

PART THREE: JESUS

12. Hope, Light, and Love   61
13. Jesus and the Good Samaritan   65
14. Jesus is Number Three   69

PART FOUR: CHRISTIANS ENTERTHE WHITE HAT – BLACK HAT WAR

15. Constantine's Legacy   73
16. Ethnic Cleansing   77
17. The Ku Klux Klan and Other Perversions of Religion   81
18. Homosexuality and Patriarchy   87

PART FIVE: CREATION STORIES

19. Coyote, Fox, and Helldiver the Duck   95
20. Pinocchio   99
21. Six Days of Creation   101

PART SIX: ADAM AND EVE: A TRADITIONAL INTERPRETATION

22. The Story's Impact on Women's Role   105
23. Men Are Meant To Control Women?   109

PART SEVEN: ADAM AND EVE NOW

24. A Symbolic Interpretation   115
25. The Serpent is a Symbol of Eternal Life,
    and of Sexual Temptation   119
26. Eve is Not a Servant for Adam,   But Represents God   121
27. Birth, Original Sin, and Butt Dust   123
28. Immersion In Love?   127
29. Birth Trauma and Baptism   129

PART EIGHT: SO WHAT CAN WE DO?

30. We Can Choose   133
31. Our Purpose in Life   137
32. Desmond Tutu: The Unlikely Power of Love and Forgiveness 143
33. Bishop Shannon: When the Cost of Being
    One of Us is Too Great   147
34. Chickens On The Highway   153
35. "GoodBye"   155
36. Afterword   157
37. Bibliography   159

Introduction

December 27, 2009

Dear Nicole,

It's your grandpa. I've been thinking about our conversation at the Mexican restaurant in Mount Vernon. You were upset that the Church and the Bible appear to condemn everyone who is not Christian, and that the Bible calls your gay friends an abomination. *"That's not right!"* you said, and you told me that you are seriously considering leaving the Church and not reading the Bible any more.

I agreed with you that the history of Christianity has included some very hateful acts against not only gay people, but also Jews, Muslims, and heretics. For you this is a very personal issue because your gay friends include some of the most compassionate, generous, loving, forgiving people you know. Maybe it is because they are victims of prejudice, but whatever the reason, many of them are more alert to the pain in other people's lives, and show their care more readily than others.

You are following your conscience by choosing love and compassion rather than judgment. I understand, and I support you. I have a friend who faces the same situation, and here is how he handles it:

I Believe in My Daughter

His daughter is gay, and he is upset that the Bible seems to condemn her. He said, "I believe in my daughter, and I believe in the Bible. But if there is a conflict, my belief in my daughter is stronger."

For him the right thing to do is to stand with his daughter. And I think it is the right thing for you to do when you choose to love your friends and to stand by them. I admire you for doing that. You are a courageous and good friend, not only for your gay friends, but also for me. And you have hit upon a very important conflict, one that I have struggled with for all of my life, a struggle that touches the heart of religious life. In fact, I have been trying to put my thoughts into a book for almost three years now, and here is my chance to write my thoughts to you, and you can let me know what you think!

The problem is this: Human beings tend to divide the world unto *us against them* as part of our instinct for *self* preservation. We need to be part of *us*, and we view *them* as a threat. In fact, being against *them* helps us bond even more with those we think of as *us*.

The Republicans view the Democrats as *them* rather than as *us,* and the Democrats reciprocate. This separates one group of Americans from another group, but it strengthens the bond Republicans have with other Republicans and the bond that Democrats have with each other. Having an opponent unites them, though at great cost to the American people.

Christians and Muslims often focus on what separates us from them rather than on what unites both groups as descendants of Abraham. Orthodox Christians have often persecuted "heretics." One gang fights another gang. We not only cheer for our team, but we want the other team to lose. At some football games we might even chant, "Hit 'em again, Hit 'em again, Harder, Harder." This is often done in fun, but it reinforces our tendency to divide into groups of *us* and *them*.

This instinct for *self* preservation is sometimes very helpful, because we need to protect ourselves from those who would hurt us. But because it creates suspicion and lack of trust this instinct is often damaging to our soul. The fear that motivates the turning against other people is often exaggerated. I think that is the reason why so many times in the Bible we are told to "Fear not," or "Be not afraid." One of my favorite books is by Dr. Jerry Jampolski called "Love is Letting Go of Fear." I think he has something important to say.

When we separate into *us* and *them* we forget that all human beings are part of *us,* created in the image of God, containing the same essence, the same DNA. We are all part of the same body. By separating into *us* and *them*, or even worse, into *us against them*, we *dismember* the body, what the Bible calls the Body of Christ, but which is also the body of human life. To dismember this body, to separate us from other human beings, is to cause *dis-ease.* It is like having an arm or a leg cut off from the body. What we must do is to *re member* this dismembered body, to put together the dismembered limbs so that we are again whole, so that the dis-ease is healed and the body is restored to health.

To re-member a separated or divided, alienated people is to restore wholeness, and to do that has a healing power. It is a work of love.

To *remember* has another meaning, of course. To remember is to recall or bring to mind information or an event that has already happened. When we do this, when we remember, the act of remembering often brings with it a partial re-experiencing of an event, stimulating some of the same emotions felt during the event. To recall or think about a joyful experience brings renewed joy. To be grateful is to remember something good in your life and to focus on its goodness. To remember an experience of love is a healing activity.

For instance: When Mary was only three years old, we lived in Northfield Minnesota where St. Olaf College is located. On a very cold winter night I was about to walk the mile from our house to the St. Olaf Campus for an evening meeting, when Mary realized I was going out into the cold. She came over and gave me a hug. "That will keep you warm," she said. I will never forget the warmth I felt at that moment, and how it not only stayed with me as I walked to campus, but how that feeling of warmth returns to me every time I think of it.

That is only one example, but there are literally hundreds of examples like that in my life. You are in some of them, and of course so are many other people – Gail, Laurie and Julie, Kyle, Justin, Aaron, and too many others to begin to list them.

I know that you have read the book I wrote about ten years ago, called "The Near Birth Experience." In that book I shared experiences of people who were taught how to remember life in the womb, before birth. Some of them were astonished that they were able to remember the safety they felt then, and that the feeling of safety was experienced again just by remembering it. Some of those people experienced the presence of God as they remembered that presence with them in the womb. Those memories were healing and helped them find meaning and purpose in life. I know you understand, because I know you experienced this for yourself some years ago. If you hadn't, I probably would not have brought it up, because for those who haven't experienced this it seems too fantastic to be real.

What I want to share with you now is what seems to be a secret for most people, but is well known among spiritual leaders. The secret is this: *Love heals the wounds of the soul.* Love, even *remembered love* heals the wounds of guilt and of the loneliness that we all experience. Love heals the separation or estrangement we experience at birth, when we are first separated from the source of our life. Love always offers an invitation to live. By the time you finish reading this, I think you will understand what I am saying, even though for you it might be a new reality.

Sometimes it is difficult to accept something new. What we have been taught helps shape our reality, and it often takes a convincing experience for us to accept something different as being real. For instance, before 1492 people thought the world was flat, so they didn't try to sail across the world; they thought they would fall off the edge if they tried. But once Columbus sailed across the world people changed their thinking, and changed their reality. Now we not only sail across the world, we fly across it.

Now we believe that the earth rotates around the sun, but because we can see with our own eyes the sun going around the world, rising and the setting, it was very difficult for people to accept that reality when Galileo and Copernicus first proposed the idea.

The Israelites once thought they were God's chosen people and nobody else mattered. That was their reality, so they thought it was okay to kill the Canaanites who lived in the "promised land," the land they thought God had promised to them. They thought that the Word of God is totally unchanging, so their reality was that barren women were cursed, that animal sacrifice is good, that heretics and idol worshippers should be put to death, and that homosexuals are an abomination to God. They thought these things because that is what the Word of God said.

But now many people have changed their thinking and believe that God is a God of love and compassion who has created all people in God's own image, and that it is God's will for us to treasure every human life. Being shaped by the first story in the Bible where human beings are created in God's image, and incorporating (taking into our very body) the words of Jesus, God's chosen people become not just the Israelites, but every human being.

What we believe is true for us; otherwise we would not believe it. What we believe is therefore "real." But something very different is "real" for someone who believes differently from us. Sometimes those different realities, those different beliefs, cause huge conflicts and great pain, often involving war and death. These different beliefs, these different "realities" cause people to separate *us* from *them*.

I am writing to encourage love not only because love offers us the best way to survive, but also because love is truly the will of God. If there is anything absolute and unchanging in the Word of God, it is that we are to love God and to love our neighbor.

I am writing to help you remember how loved you are, so that you will be continually involved in re-membering the divided and separated parts of our human family.

I am also writing because I love you – always have, always will. I want to support you, and of course I do. I smile when I am with you or think about you. I am so glad that you are going to a college near us so that we see you often. I love you *chair*.

If you don't know what that means, here is the story behind it:

Chair

When Kyle was about three or four years old, we went to watch Bevin at a gymnastics meet. I think you and your family were there too. I was sitting in the bleachers with Kyle and he said to me, "Grandpa, would you like to know how much I love you?" Of course I said yes. So he said, "If there was a snail that went all the way around the world," and he took his right hand and made a big circle to represent the trip all the way around the world, "it would take a long, long time. And if he carried something heavy it would take even longer. It would take forever! Grandpa, that's how long I would love you!"

He paused for a few seconds and then added, "You would be dead by then, but even then, I would still love you!"

When he got to be a little older, I think in the first grade, he wondered about infinity. "What is it?" he asked. When I tried to explain it, he didn't agree that infinity went on forever, and that there was no number higher than infinity. "There must be a higher number than that!" he said. "Maybe you could run out of numbers, but then you could use words. One word could mean all the numbers in infinity, and then another word could mean all the numbers after infinity. Chair, for instance, could mean all the numbers past infinity."

Then he said, "Grandpa, I love you CHAIR!"

That's how much I love you. I love you more than infinity. And I believe that God loves us that much too. God must have a lot of sadness when people turn against each other – people made in God's own image.

Gail and I are going to be in Fallbrook California for January and February, staying with Julie. I will be spending a lot of that time thinking and writing. I am writing to sort out this issue for myself, because as a pastor I run into a lot of people who think that they have to oppose gay people because the Bible seems to condemn them, or they label others as "heretics" if they believe something different from what we believe. Therefore in our eyes the "heretics" are wrong. But the issue is much wider, much greater than just the divide between gay people and heterosexuals or between Orthodox Christians and heretics.

I will be sending you my thoughts about these things, and how you and I might cure the wounds caused by the hurt other people inflict on us and the world. Not that we can cure the world, but we can help heal our own wounds, the wounds of our own soul. A very important step is to choose love, and one way to help us do that is to remember love.

Love,
Grandpa

January 4, 2010

Dear Nicole,

We are in Fallbrook. The weather here is sunny and warm at least compared to Anacortes, and I don't have any commitments here, so I will have time to focus on how to communicate my thoughts. I've decided to organize them as a book, with several parts. Part One will be about the importance of stories, because I think they are not only interesting, but can make a point without being too preachy. The rest of the book will be mostly the stories I think will explain what I have learned regarding human nature and the importance of love.

I am also going to include the ways in which religion has been misused, becoming an instrument of division rather than reconciliation and compassion for all people, along with suggestions about how to understand the reality of religion in a way more congruent with the teachings of Jesus and other spiritual leaders. I know the story of Adam and Eve will be an important part, because it has been so misused in the history of the Western World.

I'll call you to keep you up to date on my progress.

Love,
Grandpa

PART ONE: STORIES AS WISDOM

Chapter One
Stories, The Bible, and Us

When you want groceries, you go to a grocery *store*. When you want to buy new clothes, you go to a clothing store. A store is a place where things of value are *stored*. A *story* is a storehouse of wisdom, and we enter that storehouse when we hear or tell a story.

Stories are the best way I know to teach, or to get a point across. Jesus seemed to think the same thing, and that is the reason he told so many stories and parables. Much of the Bible is made up of stories, most of them to help us remember God and to remember our need for and our connection with God. Now I am going to tell you a story, a legend that condenses the message of Christianity into just a few words, words that have the power to heal our divisions and loneliness, words that have the power to heal our soul. I am going to focus on Christianity because that is part of who you are, part of who I am. The hi*story* of Christianity is a story that touches our heart and gives our soul its purpose.

John at Ephesus

John, the beloved disciple, stood at the foot of the cross when Jesus was crucified. The Bible doesn't tell us how many people were there, but we know they included a handful of women, the Roman soldiers, the mother of Jesus, and some curious people – like the ones who stop to watch as an ambulance pulls up to an accident scene. We do know that John was the only disciple there. The rest had fled; afraid they might also be arrested and crucified for being one of *them*, a disciple.

While dying on the cross, Jesus said to John, "Behold your mother." Then he said to his mother, "Behold your son." And from that day John took her under his care. They moved to Ephesus, a city that is now part of Turkey.

Ephesus was one of the first cities to have a Christian Church, due mostly to the efforts of St. Paul who preached there and later wrote a letter to the Ephesians that now is part of the Bible.

John lived in Ephesus with Mary and other Christians for several years until he was exiled to the Greek island of Patmos where he wrote the Book of Revelation. By the time he was allowed to return to Ephesus after Nero's death, he had written the Gospel of John, the Book of Revelation, and three letters contained now in the Christian Bible. He was becoming very well known as the only surviving disciple of Jesus.

The people of Ephesus wanted to hear from John what he considered to be the most important teachings of Jesus. They invited him to speak at the amphitheater, a prominent place where townspeople often gathered to see the Greek plays by Sophocles or other playwrights, or to hear important news or philosophy.

Excitement mounted as John, now over 100 years old, walked slowly to the center of the stage and took a moment to look at the thousands of people assembled to hear him. He then spoke three words in Greek: "*Teknia, agapate allylous.*" Translated into English this means, "Dear ones (or *little children*) love one another." He paused a moment and then, to everyone's amazement, slowly walked off the stage.

Dear ones, Love One Another.

These words have the power to heal our divisions, our hatreds, and our deepest wounds. They summarize the teachings of Christianity:

The first (greatest) of all commandments is this: Hear, O Israel: the Lord our God is one Lord; and you must love the Lord your God with all your heart and with all your soul and with your entire mind and with all your might; this is the first commandment.

And the second is like to it, you must love your neighbor as yourself. There is no other commandment greater than these. (Mark 12: 29-31)

When many people hear these words -- that we are to love one another, and that we are to love our neighbor as ourselves – they think that we are to love all the people we think of as one of *us*, but not to care too much about those who are *them*. Jesus meant a lot more than that, however. For him, love was the whole purpose in life. He came to remind us that we are created in the image of God, and that therefore love is of our essence. His presence and his teaching help us remember who we are and what our purpose is. His words and his presence are therefore healing, because they call to mind what love is, and they help us re-member the dismembered parts of the human family. It is important for us to know that according to Jesus the commandment to love our neighbor is like the commandment to love God. Another way to put it is that to love God is to love your neighbor, and to love your neighbor is to love God. Conversely, if you do not love your neighbor then you do not love God.

.

Aaron and 911

You and your family used to live in Bellevue when I was a pastor there, and you came to church when I preached. So Aaron heard several sermons I gave about Jesus. He was about four years old when he asked me, "Grandpa, why do you talk about Jesus so much?"

I told him that people needed to know how much God loves them, and that Jesus helped remind them of that. People often were in need of help, and God is there to help them.

He thought for a minute. "Did you ever think about having them call 911?"

He was right. People need to know not only how much God loves them; they must also be reminded how important it is to love each other and to be there to help each other. That is a very important message of Christianity.

Not only Jesus, but many other spiritual leaders have by their own lives shown the importance of loving our neighbor as well as God. Bishop Shannon and Desmond Tutu are two who have touched my life personally, but Mother Teresa and Elie Wiesel, Buddha, and Gandhi are others who come to mind. You also are one of those people who realize the importance of loving your friends and recognize that God would not want you to desert them. I believe in you. I am trying to be one of those people myself.

Justin Teaches Us a Lesson

Love is a peculiar thing. It mostly looks at the heart and what is inside a person more than it cares about outside appearances. Justin helped remind us of that on Mother's Day several years ago.

You might remember when we had two cockatiels as pets. It started out with one on Mother's Day. Your family gave your grandma a cockatiel. We went to the pet store and you all told her she could pick out any bird and they would buy it for her.

So she went to the cage where the cockatiels were, and one jumped onto her hand and walked up her arm to her shoulder. But she put it back. She said, "These birds are so expensive that I want to get the prettiest one. This one is a bit shabby, with some of its feathers pulled out."

So she chose the prettiest one.

A few hours later all of you came to our house with the first bird that had jumped onto her hand. Justin said, "Grandma, you have always said that we should look at what is in the inside of a person, not on the outside, that God looks into our hearts and we should do that too. This is the bird that loves you, that picked you. We bought it for you so it could have you."

Of course Justin was right. In a way he was helping us see that we should not make distinctions. I might be stretching it a bit, but it is a symbol also that there really is no us and them. We are all us in our hearts, on the inside. The distinctions we make that separate us are usually about outside appearances, how we look, how we talk, how we act.

So Nicole, here is a thought. The Bible does say that "God is love, and *they who abide in Love abide in God*, and God abides in them." What if God *is* Love, and believing in God is to live in the spirit of Love? If you live in love, then you are of God. Period. Regardless of whether or not you go to church, regardless whether you are straight or gay, regardless if you are black or white, Christian or Jew, *if you live in love then you are of God*. The Bible says not only that we are created in the image of God, but also *"By their fruits you shall know them."* Not by their color or their belief, but by their fruits. Do they love one another?

There is not a whole lot in this world we can control. We are all going to suffer; we are all going to die. We cannot control much of what other people do to us, whether they help us or harm us. *But it is within our control whether or not we choose to love.*

Jesus put it this way: *What does it profit a person to gain the whole world if he loses his soul?* And that is a very good question.

The problem is that sometimes, for reasons we will talk about later, we lose sight of love. We turn the world into *us against them.* But then we lose sight of the fact that every human being is created in the image of God and every person is loved by God, and that is when we lose our soul.

That is what the next chapter is about.

Chapter Two
Kindling the Sacred Fire

Ole was talking to his friend Lars about the sermon he heard at church. "The pastor said that we are all created in the image of God, and that there is a spark in our soul that could become a fire blazing with love for all people. Our job is to water that spark and make it grow!"

When we first encounter this story it seems funny. But then we realize that it points to something not so funny. Sometimes religion snuffs out the spark of love rather than fanning it into flame. Or maybe a better way to describe it is that it is our human nature that waters the spark and perverts the message of love.

Our human nature divides the world into *us against them*. The ancient Greeks called it *xenophobia*, which means that we view people who are different as a threat to us. (*Xeno* means stranger, and *phobia* means fear, being afraid of.) It is part of our instinct for *self* preservation not to trust *them*. That is the primary reason we misuse and distort the message of religion.

Religion teaches us to love *them*. Human nature makes us distrust *them*. It's pretty much that straightforward.

Unfortunately, human nature usually triumphs over religion. Stories can point this out to us, helping us see things in a new way. We begin to realize that the stories are not just about Ole and Lars or *other* people. *Every story that has meaning for us is about us.* For instance, the next story seems to be about a group of Indians who lived a long time ago. But it is really about us:

The White Hat – Black Hat War

A long time ago there were two tribes who fought about almost everything. They attacked each other's campsites to steal horses and to capture women. Whenever they encountered each other, whether on scouting expeditions, during a hunt for buffalo, or during winter migrations, they fought.

God was displeased that they fought so much, and that the destruction was so great. So one day he appeared in a vision to the chiefs and medicine men of each tribe. He said to the leaders of the first tribe: "I want you to take your people to the mesa where I will kindle a Sacred Fire. You and your people are to sit on the west side of the fire and I will appear to you with a very important message. You must obey what I say."

God also appeared to the second tribe with a similar message, except he said to them: "You and your people are to sit on the east side of the fire." So the people of both tribes gathered on the mesa, one tribe on the east side of where God had kindled the Sacred Fire, and the other tribe on the west side.

Then God appeared in the midst of the fire, and his voice was like thunder: "I am very disappointed that you are killing each other, fighting about everything, stealing from each other. I have created each of you and I love you all. You are all my people. You must no longer think of each other as enemies. Be at peace with each other. This message is my most important teaching, and I give it to you now as my Greatest Commandment: *You must love one another.*"

But as God spoke, the people noticed that he was wearing a hat. One side of the hat, the side facing east, was white, and the side facing west was black. So the people on the east side of the fire thought God had a white hat on his head, and the people on the west thought God's hat was black.

After God had given his commandments, He disappeared from sight. That is when the people began to disagree about the color of God's hat. The tribe on the east insisted it was *White*, the tribe on the west insisted it was *Black*. And thus began The Great Hat Color War that nearly destroyed both tribes.

That story pretty much describes how some people have responded to the Word of God, by ignoring the message of love and dividing the world into *us against them*. Homosexuals, heretics, Jews, Muslims, African Americans, American Indians, and others have been persecuted just because they are different from *us* in some way. That makes them *them,* not one of *us.* That makes it easy for disagreements to turn into war, and God's message of love gets lost even for devout Christians.

But here is the thing: If we think that religion teaches us to hate other people, then it is our instinct for *self* preservation that has perverted the message. It is our instinct for self preservation that makes us believe that having the best army and the most powerful weapons is the best way to survive, that love is not as powerful as rifles and weapons of warfare. The reason America is no longer a nation divided into Indian tribes instead of states is that the U.S. Calvary had better weapons than the bow and arrow.

We have to agree that war has worked in the past, for the Romans and for all other empires, including the United States. Yet most of these empires have fallen because eventually they were defeated. It is time to learn from them. In this modern world of nuclear, biological, and chemical weapons, we have to learn a better way or we could destroy the whole world. Or someone with nuclear bombs could destroy *us.* There are very few nations we could fight who still have only the bow and arrow.

Christianity teaches a better way, and so do other religions. Of the six most influential people in the history of the world, five are religious leaders, according to a book by Michael Hart, a book we will look at later. There is a reason for this. Love is the most important thing in the world, and religions teach love. The main problem is that it is very difficult to live according to the teaching. That is not the fault of the teaching, but of those who distort the teaching, like the people gathered on the mesa who focused on the color of God's hat instead of paying attention to the message of love, or the people who water the spark of love with the hope that they will make it grow into a flame.

There are two ways to respond to this widespread turning the message of love into *us against them* behaviors. One way is to just say, "I don't want to have anything to do with such hypocrisy. I'm out of here!" That is a very tempting thing to do. But there is another way, one that takes a great deal of courage, but is the way taken by some of the greatest people on earth: *To call people back to the message of love.*

That might not be as hard as it seems, because people already have love for those they think of as one of *us*. Many if not most people will give their very lives for those who are family or in the case of the military, those who are of our country.

What needs to happen is to take the next step: To view all human beings as *us* and to love all human beings as part of the same family. If we are not able to do that, some terrible things can happen. John Wilkes Booth, for instance, thought he was doing a great thing by assassinating President Lincoln. He had been listening too much to the people of the South who thought Lincoln was becoming a dictator, and he thought people all over the country would rise up against Lincoln's government and would see that Booth was a hero for killing him and setting things right. He had no idea that he was making things worse, both for the North and for the South. It is possible for people even now to do terrible things with horrible consequences, while at the same time thinking they are doing the right thing.

In a class you took preparing you to be an elementary schoolteacher, one of your assignments was to tell a story as if you were telling it to first or second graders. You liked that assignment, and you practiced telling me the story of *He who holds the sky with both hands*. The moral of the story is that people are created in the image of their creator, so they should act more godlike, more loving towards each other and not forget who they are. So that is what we will look at now. That message can be a great help for the world.

Chapter Three
He Who Holds the Sky With Both Hands

He Who Holds the Sky made the world, and it was a grand and wonderful creation. He made graceful animals like the deer and the antelope and the gazelle. He made majestic birds like the eagle, and beautiful birds like the hummingbirds with iridescent feathers that reflect the sun as they zoom up, down, or in any direction, able to hover and then suddenly zip away. He made roses and other fragrant and beautiful flowers. He made peacocks and butterflies and whales, and everything beautiful and majestic; but the pride of his creation was human beings, who were made in his own image and likeness, beings who were given life by having the breath and the spirit of He Who Holds the Sky with Both Hands breathed into their innermost being. When he looked at his creation, he said, "This is very good!" And he smiled, and then rested.

But he had a younger brother, whose name was Flint (in some versions his name is Ice.) Flint was jealous of his brother. He tried to make things as wonderful as his brother had made, but his attempt to make a graceful gazelle emerged as a frog. It could jump, but was no gazelle. And when Flint tried to make an eagle, a buzzard appeared. It was big but no eagle. When he tried to make a hummingbird, what emerged was a bumblebee that could hum or buzz like a hummingbird, but was not beautiful. His try at a butterfly ended up as a mosquito. Even his attempt to make a flower turned into thistles and nettles.

So Flint was jealous. He couldn't do much, but he had been given one power, a curse. He had only one curse, so he had to be sparing in its use. He decided to use it to curse human beings, who were the pride of his brother's creation, beings so much like his brother, the brother he envied so much. His curse was that humans would forget who they were, would forget in whose image they were created.

And so because of the curse, humans forgot that they were in the image and likeness of their creator. Forgetting their noble nature, their holy nature, they began to act in ways that were not attractive or noble.

They began to have wars, to not care for the sick, to neglect the old and the poor.

So the world became less beautiful, less loving. That is when He Who Holds the Sky with Both Hands began to grieve. This was not turning out the way he wanted. Finally, after many years he decided to do something.

He came down to earth, and paused at the teepee of one of the most cruel of all humans, one who acted only for his own selfish ends, one who neglected all others as if they were not his brothers or sisters. He Who Holds the Sky with Both Hands climbed to the top of this man's tepee and looked down through the smoke hole. He saw the man stirring a pot of stew.

When the man looked into the pot of stew what he saw was the reflection in the water of He Who Holds the Sky with Both Hands, and he thought it was his own reflection. In a way he was right, for he was truly made in the image of his creator. But it was a shock to him. "If this is the way I look, then I'm not living up to my appearance," he thought. "My reflection is of nobility, of honor and integrity, even holiness. It is so awesome and inspiring to look that way, it might be just as awesome and inspiring to act that way." So he began to act in accordance with his new vision of self, a vision of his true self long forgotten but now awakened, now remembered.

For many years he and his children and then his children's children acted with nobility, and they inspired others to do the same. But then the forgetting began again and as the years went by humans became less human. He Who Holds the Sky with Both Hands began to grieve again. He thought and he thought. Then he decided, "I know what to do. I will send my son. He will teach them, and they will remember."

So he sent his son, and many lives were changed by him, both by his example and by his teachings. Many humans began to act with nobility again and even with grace and love. They again reflected his light, and by being more like who they were created to be, they lived with more joy.

Think about it. When you do something that you know is right, when you act with love for someone, don't you feel a lot better? Think about the time you helped a second grader at the playground when you stopped a fourth grader from bullying him. You knew that you did the right thing, and one of the kids on the playground said it was a great thing for him to see you keep the playground safe.

Well, that is what happened for those who remembered and who lived according to the wishes of their creator. They not only felt better, but they acted in ways to re-member the isolated parts of their tribe so that dis-membered parts could come together into the same body. They began to live with more love, more safety.

But many did not accept such a life. There were those who lived the way of love, and those who lived the way of self. Even now it remains to be seen if the divided parts can be re-membered.

There are several versions of this story, which is true of many legends that come to us from a time or from a people who did not have these stories written down but instead told them around a campfire or when it was time to put the children to bed. This version is one that originated in the Onondaga Indian tribe and I have listed the source in the bibliography. But in all the versions that I have heard, a central message of this story is the same one as the theme of the plaque you gave me for Christmas:

To love someone is to learn the song in their heart and to sing it to them when they have forgotten.

It is very important to remember who we are, and other people can help by reflecting to us that we are good, created in the image of God. When we forget, they can remember the song in our heart and sing it to us. That is our job as human beings. Of course there are many ways to do that.

You know I believe that all of us were with God before we were born, and that we came to this earth with a purpose. We had the choice. We could stay with God in Heaven or we could do something to bring love and the presence of Grace to this place. The trouble is that even though we have this deeply buried memory of who we are and who God is, we forget. We have a loneliness for God, but we don't always recognize what the loneliness is. It is as St. Augustine said, *Our hearts were made for Thee, O God, and cannot rest until they rest in Thee.*

Well, that is the reason this story of He Who Holds the Sky is so important. Its message is that we should never forget who we are, a person created in the image of God. When we remember that, it helps us be more of who we are meant to be, a light in the darkness, a mirror that reflects love. This is so important that it is too bad it is sometimes a very hard thing to do. Fortunately, there are people around us who can help.

Of course this story is symbolic. Its message is that the most important job parents have is to keep reminding their children that they are precious, valued and treasured. That helps them live as people of value, created in the image of God. Remembering this helps them be good.

The story of He Who Holds the Sky is a lot like the very first story in the Bible. Both stories teach that people are created in the image of God; they are created as "very good," and so they should act that way. This is a message people need to hear over and over again, and the job of religion is to remind us in every way possible that we need to love each other.

That is one of the reasons I am glad you are learning to be a teacher. You will continue to be such a great help to your students, encouraging them to live life as people of immense value. You will listen to the song of their hearts and you will sing it back to them. They will grow to love you, and you will be a wonderful influence for their lives.

But now, here is something to think about. This story of He Who Holds the Sky is obviously very close to the message of Christianity, that we are created in the image of God, but sometimes we forget and act less than holy, so that God's son came to remind us who we are.

So Nicole, think about this: What if it is *really true* that someone came from God to give us a message about how important love is, and what if it really matters if we listen to that message? What if even the Church forgets that love is the soul of Christianity and of all religion, and what if even the religious people begin to act as if God wants us to live as *us against them* instead of *We are all us*? What if Christians turn against Muslims or Jews, or if white people turn against people who are not white? If that happens, what are we to do?

What Jesus did is this: He lived a life of love for all people, even though he was killed because he loved not only *us*, but also *them*. This might be difficult, but I believe that is what we should do.

Of course a person can live in love without being part of the Christian Church. Sometimes the Church gets in the way. But before we look at that, I want to look at one of the messages of He Who Holds the Sky: that *we must reflect to other people that they are in the image of God*.

There is a religion, I think Buddhist, but it might be Hindu, where when people meet they put the palms of their hands together and bow to each other and say, "Namaste!" The greeting signifies, "The soul, or spirit of goodness that is within me recognizes and honors the good that is within you." It can be a very meaningful encounter.

We have rituals that can be meaningful like that, but sometimes we act as if they are just commonplace. For instance, when you and I are talking on the phone and the conversation is finished, we might say, "Goodbye grandpa" and "Goodbye Nicole." And when we do, it can signify what it originally did, "God be with Ye." (*Ye* was an old way of saying *you*.) It was a blessing. And it can be still. Remember that the next time you say "goodbye," or the next time someone says "goodbye" to you.

It is of interest to me that the two words *inspire* and *expire* originally meant "to breathe In" and "to breathe out." But the word "inspire" also means to encourage or to motivate someone to greater effort, to cause enthusiasm. And the word "expire" means to die or to perish. I mention this because I think that if we do not inspire someone, or if we are not inspired by someone, then we expire, we die, or at least an important part of our soul dies.

The point is that we need to reflect goodness to each other, to inspire others to see their goodness, to help them understand that they are created in the image of God, so that when they look in a mirror, or in the mirror of what we and other people reflect to them, they see something good. This is important, because what we see influences what we get.

Chapter Four
What You See is What You Get

Once there was a dog who went to the state fair. Well, you've been to the Puyallup, so you know how crowded it can get at the state fair. That's what happened. He was in such a crowd that he was afraid he would get stepped on, so he ducked into a doorway and found himself in a Hall of Mirrors.

I'm not sure if you know what a Hall of Mirrors is. It is a place where there are about a hundred mirrors, but they are not ordinary mirrors. Some of them make you look fat, some make you look skinny. Some make you look very tall, and some make you look very short. They distort your reflection in every way you can think of.

So, this dog looked and saw about a hundred different dogs, some short, some tall, some fat, some skinny, and so on. Well, it frightened him a bit to see all those dogs looking at him, so he decided to scare some of them away. He barked and growled and even snarled at them. But it made him even more scared when they all barked and growled and snarled right back at him. He was so scared that he turned around and ran, but when he looked back to see if any of them were chasing him, he discovered that they had all run away from him, and now they were looking back to see if he was following them!

So he relaxed a bit, and even smiled, quite proud of himself for scaring all those dogs that outnumbered him so much. To his surprise, they all smiled back, so he wagged his tail and slowly walked toward them, figuring he had made about a hundred new friends. And of course, they did the same.

It is very important what other people reflect to us, but that is not the only important factor in how we see ourselves and how we view the world. We can see the world differently depending on *what we choose to focus on*. How we view life has an impact even on our health.

Attitude of Gratitude.

Ten days after my dad died, my mother -- your great grandmother -- had a massive heart attack. We thought she would die, but after several crises she pulled through. On the day she was discharged the cardiologist who was in charge of her care at the hospital came to see her. My brother Tom and my sisters Cindy and Carol were with me when I heard him tell her:

"Juel, I know you will take care of yourself and get some exercise and take your medications every day. That is important. But the most important thing is something not everyone knows, so I want you to listen carefully. The most significant thing I have observed for people recovering from a heart attack is an ***attitude of gratitude***.

"Every morning when you wake up, before you get up, I want you to think of something you are grateful for. And at least three times a day find something else to be thankful for. That is the attitude that will help you get well, and it my most important prescription for you."

This advice seems to have worked for her. She is now 92. She is frail, but her attitude brightens the room and is often commented on by those who live in the same building. When I go to St. Paul to see her, many of the people in the building will say something like, "Juel is my best friend here. She is always so happy and kind." I think that what has happened for her is that she is able to remember the good things, and that has a healing power.

Anne Frank

Instead of looking at the negative, we can develop, all of us, an attitude of gratitude, or a positive attitude toward life. One of the most influential inspirational books of all time is Anne Frank's diary. Living in Nazi-occupied Holland as a Jew, she had a lot to complain about. But instead she wrote this in her diary just a few days before she was captured and sent to a concentration camp: (You can get her diary at any library. It's called *The Diary of a Young Girl*. Any librarian will help you.)

It's really a wonder that I haven't dropped all my ideals, because they seem so absurd and impossible to carry out. Yet I keep them, **because in spite of everything I still believe that people are really good at heart.**

I simply can't build up my hopes on a foundation consisting of confusion, misery, and death. I see the world gradually being turned into a wilderness. I hear the ever approaching thunder, which will destroy us too. I can feel the sufferings of millions and yet, if I look up into the heavens, I think that it will all come right, that this cruelty too will end, and that peace and tranquility will return again. In the meantime I must uphold my ideals, for perhaps the time will come when I shall be able to carry them out.

Saturday, 15 July, 1944

She died later at Bergen-Belsen concentration camp, but her view of life has influenced and inspired millions of people who recognized the basic truth of her message. The people of the world could not support what the Nazis did. In the end, Anne Frank's idealism survived but the Nazis did not. There is something so pervasive that it cannot die, and that is our desire for the good. Eventually that is what must triumph, or else we will all perish. The job of religion, and our purpose in life, is to see that the good triumphs.

So that's enough for now. In our next chapter our focus will be on the beginning of Christianity and its roots in the Jewish religion, the religion of the Israelites who are also known as the Hebrews.

Meanwhile, "Goodbye" Nicole!

Chapter Five
Remembering Who We Are

A long time ago, before there were any books and before anyone knew how to read, when television was thousands of years in the future and when there wasn't very much to do when it got dark, people told stories. Sometimes they sat around a campfire like you did when you were a campfire girl, but sometimes mom or dad told stories to their children before they went to sleep. Some of the stories were about how the world was created, or how Noah and all the animals of the earth survived a huge flood, or how the people of Israel came to live in Egypt for 400 years. These stories are now part of the Bible, but they were not written down until the time of Moses, and then other stories were added as over a thousand years went by, till finally the whole Bible was written.

The stories became very important to the Hebrew people when they were slaves in Egypt. The stories helped them know who they were, giving them an identity, telling them how they were different from the Egyptians and other people, identifying who is *us* and who is *them*

We are going to look at some of these stories in Chapter Six when we focus on the beginning of the Bible and our religion. But first I want to tell you a story about you and the first time we ever noticed how worship was such a spontaneous part of you. I think awe and wonder are part of the soul of every person. For sure that is true of you. This story tells a lot about who you are.

Awe and Wonder at the Beach

You were only eighteen months old, and you and your mom and dad and Justin and Aaron were visiting us when we lived in West Seattle by the beach. We were walking along on the sand and you were barefoot and you held your grandma's hand as you let the waves splash over your feet.

You looked at the setting sun and the Olympic Mountains, and you started to sing, and to dance. You were making up the words which weren't really words, and the dance was a great spontaneous dance, and it was awesome. You were worshipping God and the beauty of it all, or at least that is how it seemed to us. The joy just seemed to spill out of you. It was a magic moment for your grandma and me, a spiritual time I will never forget. I have decided to put a picture of you running on the beach two years later as the cover of what will be this book. It will help you and me remember a time of joy, one of the many times of joy in our lives.

You are still that same enthusiastic person, now a young woman. I use the word "enthusiastic" because it has a meaning we sometimes forget. It is a word that comes from the Greek language: "*En Theos*," a person who lives "In God." That is pretty much the topic of the stories I am about to tell you – some of them will be very familiar, and some you may not have heard yet. They are about God, people, the Bible, and how our spiritual nature often fights with our more selfish nature, the part of us that is about *self* preservation.

As long as I have already mentioned the conflict between our spiritual nature and our more selfish nature, I might as well tell you a story about that.

The Lakota Chief and a Young Warrior

Before the Europeans came to America there was a large tribe of Native Americans who called themselves the *Lakota*. They lived in the Midwest, in places that are now called North and South Dakota. The Lakota also were known by the white man as the Sioux Indians.

One day a Lakota warrior came to his chief. "I have a problem," he said. "I want to do what is right, but sometimes it seems that there are two wild dogs fighting inside me. One of them agrees with me, that I should do the right thing, but the other dog snarls and pulls me in the other direction, towards what I know is wrong. The problem is that there is always something very tempting, very appealing in that direction, and sometimes that is what I do."

"That is a common problem among people," said the chief. "Usually what is tempting has to do with sex or greed or something that makes us feel pleasure or gives us power. Even when we know that the right thing is in the other direction, sometimes the temptation is so powerful that we give in to it. We let the wrong dog lead us.

"So here is what to do.

"The dog you feed will become strong, and the dog you starve will get weak."

The chief didn't explain any more than that, but the warrior knew what he meant.

Chapter Six
Abraham, Monotheism and the Bible

Now we are going to look at some of the first stories of our history, the first stories of our Bible. We will start with Abraham because before Abraham there was no Bible. Abraham is the ancestor not only of Christianity, but also of Judaism and Islam. These important world religions have these three things in common:

1. They all view Abraham as the first Patriarch of their religion;
2. Each of these religions worships only one God (Religions that worship only one god are called monotheistic religions, a combination of two Greek words: *Mono* means "one" and *Theos* means "god.")
3. They believe that God is male.

Abraham and Idols

In his book about Abraham (see the bibliography), Bruce Feiler tells this story, one passed on from parent to child:

Abraham lived in Ur of the Chaldeans where people worshipped many gods. They would make clay images of these gods, and would worship these idols. Abraham's father Terah kept some of these idols in his tent. One day Abraham took a stick and smashed one of the idols sitting on a shelf with some other idols, and when Terah saw the smashed idol he was very angry. "Come here, Abe!" he said. "I am going to have to punish you for doing this." And Terah picked up a stick.

But Abraham said, "Father, I didn't do it! This other idol sitting on the shelf pushed that idol and it fell to the ground and broke!"

Terah raised his stick when he heard this, and was about to beat Abraham with it. "You lie!" he said. "You know those idols are just made of clay! Look at the broken one! It's just pieces of clay lying on the ground! That other idol is also made of clay and certainly could not have done this!"

Then Abraham said to his father, "If they are only made out of clay and cannot do anything, then why do you worship them?"

The parents would then tell their children, "That was the beginning of our religion, the worship of the One True God! It began when Abraham realized that the worship of idols was foolish."

It is true that there is only one God, but what does that mean? It does *not* mean that everyone has to believe the same thing or look the same or be just like us. God is one, and has created us in God's image, but yet we are made wonderfully diverse. When we say that God is one, what it means is that God is Love. If what you do is of love, it is of God. Everyone who loves is doing the will of God, and God dwells in that person because God is Love. And yet there are many diverse ways of living in love.

By knowing this, we can strive to live in love, because then we are living in the Spirit of God. Love unites us, with each other and with God. Love makes us whole, makes us one despite our diversity. There are many who are different from us, and yet are not a threat to us. The problem is that it is hard to separate who is a threat from who is not.

When Christians killed heretics, they were not acting out of love. They were killing people who were different, and they thought that if they were different they were not one of *us* and were therefore a threat. Christians felt the same way when they were part of the Crusades against the Jews or Muslims, and they do the same thing when they judge gay and lesbian people. They are afraid that these people are a threat.

Our misunderstanding has been partly due to our understanding of what is called "patriarchal" religion. Patriarchal religion encourages division into us against them, and it encourages having one strong male leader, usually a king or pharaoh or emperor or pope. If that strong leader views someone different as a threat, then the whole country or tribe follows the leader. This can and does lead to war and ethnic cleansing.

Abraham and Patriarchal Religion

Before Abraham, there were many gods and goddesses worshipped by ancient peoples. Clay figurines (what we have called idols) have been found by archeologists. Some were of females with large breasts and wide hips that were associated with Mother Earth. But these were an abomination to the patriarchs, including Abraham and his descendants. Patriarchy means "rule by men, or a society where men (the fathers) are the most powerful members." Christianity is both a monotheistic religion believing there is only one God, a God of Love; and it is also (or has been) a patriarchal religion, believing (up until very recently) that men should rule and women should be submissive. Monotheism and patriarchy are two different things, but Judaism, Christianity, and Islam have combined these two things. They worship One God, and men rule.

Abraham's name points the way to honoring *men*. *Ab* means "father." The name *Ab*raham means "father of many nations," and God is believed to be male. Jesus uses the name *Abba* to refer to God as "Daddy" or "Father," and in early Christianity, in fact up until about the lifetime of my grandparents, it remained a patriarchal religion where *only men* were bishops, popes, and part of the hierarchy, the rulers of the Church. This happened because the church believed that only men were in the image of God. They forgot that male and female were both created in God's image.

Abraham, Sarah, and *Yits Ha Ha*c

Abraham and his wife Sarah lived about 3700 years ago in a society that highly valued children, especially male children. Children were needed to help watch the flocks, usually sheep and goats, and they were also important to the tribe as members who could fight and defend them from their enemies as they reached adulthood.

Though the people were tough and strong, many children died before they were five years old, and many women died in childbirth. So people tried to have large families. Women who did not produce any children were called "barren," like a wasteland that doesn't have any life.

Abraham and Sarah were in their nineties and had given up on having a child. So Abraham took his slave Hagar and had a child with her! The name of that child was Ishmael. But then, as if by a miracle, Abraham and Sarah had a son. Sarah laughed when they had that baby, so they named him *Isaac*. They pronounced that name as "Yits *ha ha* c," which sounds a bit like a person laughing. And that's what the name Isaac means, in Hebrew: "laughter."

Abraham became the father, or ancestor, of many peoples. His son Ishmael became the father of the Arab tribes; Ishmael's half-brother Isaac became the father of Jacob, who became a patriarch (the father, or leader) of the Hebrews.

Jacob

One of the stories the mom or dad would tell had to do with the history of their people after Abraham died. As the children gathered around, the story would begin, much like when an elementary schoolteacher gathers the children around, and then she (or he) begins the story.

Children, this is the story of Jacob, the son of Isaac, who was the son of Abraham. Jacob had 12 sons, and each of these sons became the head (or Patriarch) of one of the 12 tribes of *Israel*.

Do you children ever wonder why we are known as the 12 tribes of *Israel*, if we are the sons of *Jacob*?

The answer is this: One day Jacob spent the night wrestling with God, or possibly with an angel. That was an important time for him, and so he changed his name to Israel, which means "one who wrestles with God." As children of Israel we are also called Israelites. We also wrestle with God.

Nicole, you and I are like those Israelites. We also wrestle with God, or at least with the way religion sometimes portrays God.

Moses and the Beginning of the Written Bible

There are other stories in the Book of Genesis, the longest one being about Joseph, a son of Jacob who was sold into slavery in Egypt. The Hebrews then spent 400 years there, until Moses led them out of slavery into the freedom of the "Promised Land." The story of Moses begins in the second book of the Bible, the Book of Exodus.

The very first words *written* in the Bible were written on two tablets of stone after Moses led the Israelites out of slavery. Up until that time the stories that are now part of the Bible were not written, but were part of what we call the *oral tradition*. They were stories many of the Hebrews knew by heart, but there was no book called the Bible, until Moses.

Moses came to Mount Sinai, went up to the top of the mountain for 40 days, and came down with the two tablets. Carved on these stone tablets were the 10 Commandments, the Sacred Words of God that were kept in the *Ark of the Covenant*. A few years ago there was a movie about Indiana Jones searching for that ark, and you might have seen that movie.

During about the next thousand years or so the rest of the Hebrew Bible was written, the part of the Bible that Christians sometimes refer to as the "Old Testament."

The people of Israel had now defined themselves. They were people descended from Abraham, people who worshipped the God of Moses, people who accepted the laws of the 10 Commandments. They were *us*. Everybody else was *them*.

Joshua and Ethnic Cleansing

Joshua was a warrior who took control of the Israeli army after Moses died, about 3300 years ago.

(Nicole, when I say that Moses died about 3300 years ago, that is approximate. Scholars think that is about right, but it is hard to be sure. It reminds me of the story of the museum guide when the group he was leading came to the dinosaur exhibit.

"These bones in this dinosaur skeleton are two million and four years old," he said. Someone asked him how he could be so precise, so exact about the dating of something so old.

"Well, I started work here four years ago, and then I was told they were two million years old! You do the math!")

Joshua conquered most of the land of Canaan, believing that it was God's will, that God had promised the land to Abraham and his descendants. He also believed it was God's will that many of the tribes he conquered should be slaughtered – the men, women, children, and even their animals. Otherwise there would be remnants that could eventually cause trouble for the Israelites. He also smashed the temples and idols worshipped by the pagan peoples. This is one of the first acts of ethnic cleansing committed by the Israelites, an act of *us against them*. The Israelites and the monotheistic religion now ruled, and Joshua was their leader.

The name *Joshua* is the same name, in Hebrew, as *Jesus*. As time went by the Jews waited for a promised Messiah, a new Joshua who would defeat their enemies, including the Roman legions, so that Jerusalem and Israel would replace the Roman Empire. All nations would then pay tribute and they will rule the earth, under God. When Jesus indicated that he was the awaited Messiah, they expected that he would be a warrior like his namesake, Joshua.

But he disappointed them. He challenged their understanding of God, of the Bible, and of the role of the Messiah by giving his life in service to others rather than taking the role of a warrior king. He promoted baptism rather than circumcision as a way for a person to be brought into a new covenant with God. This allowed women to become full members of the household of believers, whereas formerly only men could participate fully in God's covenant established by circumcision. Jesus changed the patriarchal religion of Abraham, the understanding of the role of the Messiah, and the role or the status of women and introduced what Christians now call the "New Covenant," or the "New Testament."

God's Name and Titles

The Israelites were the first to believe that there is only One God, and they knew his name: *Yahweh.* That was God's *name,* but they also called Him by titles, like *God, almighty God, God of Abraham,* and others. Sometimes they just referred to God as *The Name* (in Hebrew, *Ha Shem*) because the name of God was so holy that it seemed a sacrilege for an ordinary human to pronounce it.

The Hebrews now had an identity as the people who worshipped the God of Abraham, who obeyed the 10 Commandments, and who knew God's name. They were *us.*

BUT:

Everyone else was *them.* So the Hebrews killed *them* and took their land. After all, God was with *us,* **not** with *them.*

The problem is that even now many people think the same way. We tend to think that all of those who are part of *us* are important, but those who are *them* are not very important

Even Christians fall into this trap, despite the fact that Jesus preached over and over again that we should love *every* person as one of *us.* That is a very hard thing to do, so most of us live in a world that is much too small. Recently this came to our attention again when President Obama said he was a citizen of the world, but a lot of people criticized him and said, "We are Americans, *not* citizens of the world!" These people are a lot like the frog in the following story:

The Frog in the Well

Once there was a frog who lived in a well. He was born there and had never left the well. Every day he ate the worms and algae and kept the water pure and clean for himself and for the humans who drew water from the well.

One day another frog who lived in the sea came and fell into the well.

"Where are you from?"

"I am from the sea."

"The sea? What is that? Where is that? Is it as big as my well?"

He took a leap from one side of the well to the other.

"The sea is much greater than your well."

The frog took another leap. "Is your sea this big?"

The second frog laughed. "The sea is so much bigger than your well that it is ridiculous to compare the two!"[1]

(This story is in a book called *the Complete Works of Swami Vivekananda*. I've listed it in the bibliography.)

One reason people go to war, one reason why even religious people learn to hate and kill other people, is that they live in a very small world, like the first frog. They might love those they think of as *us,* but they don't care much about *them.* That is the topic of the next chapters where we look at psychology as well as theology. After all, we are human beings and we need to understand human behavior.

PART TWO: HUMAN NATURE

Chapter Seven
We Need to be One of Us

We need to belong. It is the reason gangs have initiation rites, why the military submits recruits to the indignities of boot camp, why primitive tribes have painful rites of passage, and why some colleges and even high schools have hazing rituals. You are one of *us* if you are willing to endure physical or psychological pain in order to belong to our group. If you are one of us, you can count on us to be there for you. If you are one of us, you might dress in a way that shows you are part of the group, part of the gang. It is the reason you might wear a sweatshirt that says "Western Washington University." That sweatshirt says you are one of *us* when you are on campus.

To be one of us is a great thing: To cheer for *our* team, to be proud of our country, to salute our flag. But sometimes to be one of us comes at a cost that is too high to pay.

Murder in West Seattle

One morning when we lived in West Seattle, we looked out our window and saw a park bench by the beach, covered with flowers. We soon discovered that two people had been shot. They had been sitting on that park bench at about 11:00 the night before when a car pulled up close to them and someone fired two shots. The woman died immediately from a bullet to her head. The man survived, shot in the eye. The flowers were to pay tribute to this couple.

The man who survived was able to give enough information to the police that they were able to catch the young man who shot them. He had been part of a gang initiation, and needed to kill somebody in order to become a gang member. He did not know the woman he killed or the man who lost the sight of his eye, but he was willing to kill in order to become a member of the gang. He would have done almost anything to be a member of the gang, a member of us. The price he was willing to pay was very high. Too high.

The need to be one of *us* is so powerful that almost any military organization, almost any gang, almost every country, can count on it. Gang members typically wear gang colors or tattoos to identify that they are now one of *us*. The military has uniforms, and each branch of the service is a separate unit. The marines think they are best, and they are faithful to one another. *Semper Fi*. The Special Forces think they are best. The Air Force is above it all. If you wear our uniform, you are one of *us*, you will put yourself in harm's way to protect anyone else who is one of *us* – and those who are *us* will do the same for you.

Clever advertisers use *the need to be us* to their advantage. They label the clothes that become the uniform for the *in crowd*. If you don't wear these designer jeans or those shoes you might not be one of *us*. When Julie was a teenager she wanted to wear "James Jeans," because they were the "in thing." And as the "in thing," they cost twice as much as other jeans. Holden Caulfield explains it this way, explaining his choice of roommates in the book "Catcher in the Rye." That was a very popular book when I was in college, and if you haven't read it yet you can borrow my copy. In my opinion, it is well worth reading.

Holden Caulfield

The thing is, it's really hard to be roommates with people if your suitcases are much better than theirs -- if yours are really good ones and their's aren't. You think if they're intelligent and all, the other person, and have a good sense of humor, that they don't give a damn whose suitcases are better, but they do. They really do. It's one of the reasons why I roomed with a stupid bastard like Stradlater. At least his suitcases were as good as mine. (Excuse the language)

We all started out as being one of us. All we had to do was to be born into a loving family. (Some mothers do not keep their babies, but anyone old enough to read this, and that includes you, have been loved or you would not be alive. You would have died if you were not loved.) A mother accepts her newborn baby not only because the baby has been in her womb for approximately nine months, and not only because now the baby attaches itself to her when it nurses, but also because the baby has the same genes. It will resemble its parents. The baby may be a newcomer but it is not a stranger, it is already familiar. It is *like* us. We are genetically programmed to protect this child, this genetic reservoir who will pass our genes on to the next generation. We love this child because it is one of *us*.

But eventually having the same genes is not enough. We will need to act and think in ways that are acceptable to our group. For instance,

A Leaky Roof

I spent a summer living with an Austrian family as an exchange student when I was in high school. Austria was a Catholic country and everyone in our village in the Tyrolean Alps went to mass on Sunday. One Sunday while we were walking to church after a rain that had lasted all day Saturday, we saw a man on his roof with a hammer, repairing a leak. A large crowd had gathered around his house, and people were chanting that he should not be working but should be at church. It was Sunday, a day of rest and worship. According to Catholic teaching, it is a mortal sin to not attend mass on Sunday. Soon he came down from the roof and joined the crowd. He wanted to be one of us, and that meant following the rules. So he went to church.

Jerusalem or Mecca?

When Muhammad first established his new religion of Islam, he believed that the three monotheistic patriarchal religions descended from Abraham had so much in common that they would be allies. They were all us.

This is a great idea, but it didn't last long. He told his people to face Jerusalem when they prayed, to honor and be in solidarity with the first two religions of the book, because for each of these three religions Jerusalem was a holy city, the city of David and of Jesus. But when Muhammad discovered that Christians and Jews were fighting with each other, and that neither of these religions accepted him or his new revelation, he reversed his thinking. They were no longer us, but them. To symbolize his change of heart, he had his followers face Mecca rather than Jerusalem when they prayed. Ever since then the relationship has been strained between Muslims and Jews and Christians.

It is so important to be one of *us* that it can even be a matter of life and death. That is what the following chapter is about.

Chapter Eight
It Can Be a Matter of Life and Death

To be one of us can be a matter of life and death not only for the people who are *them,* people who might be thought of as the enemy. It is also a matter of life and death for those who are one of us.

If you do not give in to the pressure to live by the rules of the group, you might find out that you are no longer one of us, and in some cases this can be deadly. **To be one of *us* is a matter of survival**. If there is no one to feed us and care for us during our first years of life, we will die. Even as adults we need to be part of a group, to be connected with those who know us, love us, respect us, and will protect us. A man without a country, a person without friends, or a prisoner in solitary confinement will find life lonely and of little value. Solitary confinement has been called a cruel and unusual punishment, and living without love is enormously stressful. We need to have an invitation to live, a sense that we belong, that we are valued. We need to share our joy when we are happy, and when we are sad we need someone to share our burden. Without family or country, without someone who cares about us, life loses its meaning.

Dr. Walter Bradford Cannon of Harvard Medical School wrote an article explaining how this can happen. Maybe you studied this in a psychology class. He described many examples of healthy young adults who died within a few days after they were "hexed" by a voodoo witch doctor in various remote places in South America, Africa, Australia, New Zealand, Haiti, and islands in the South Pacific.

Voodoo

Dr. Cannon discovered that black magic probably didn't have anything to do with the deaths, and there was no sign of violence. He believed they were scared to death. Once the word of their hexing was out, the victims were often abandoned by their tribe and even by their families, who were afraid they might be next if they stayed with the victim. The stress of no longer being one of *us* was so great that the fear, *caused by the loss of social support*, led to the death of the person who was "hexed." Without social support, life loses much of its meaning.

That is why it is so important to reflect to each person how valuable they are, and how much we benefit from them. Everyone needs an invitation to live. If a person is not appreciated, if a person feels like he or she is a burden, if a person feels alienated from those who are *us*, then life becomes a struggle. That is one of the reasons some gay and lesbian people, why some veterans of the Vietnam conflict who did not feel appreciated or honored for their sacrifice, (officially that was not a war, just a conflict; but for those who fought, it was a war) and why some people going through a divorce might find themselves contemplating suicide. Even a soldier like Julius Caesar, according to Shakespeare, will give up when he feels betrayed by his friends (Brutus, for instance). We need to be one of *us*. That is the message of the next story, of a soldier in the Civil War. (Of course I realize that no war is Civil, just as no war is Holy. But that's what we call it, the Civil War – the war between states.)

General Richard Garnett

General Richard Garnett was a graduate of West Point who resigned his commission in the Union Army when he learned that the South had seceded from the Union. He considered the South to be one of *us* and the North to be *them*. He was commissioned as a Brigadier General in the Confederate Army and served under Lt. General Stonewall Jackson.

On March 23, 1862 he led an attack on the Union forces at Kernstown, and after two hours of combat with superior numbers of Union troops attacking from three directions, Garnett's command began to run low on ammunition because the supply wagons had been left behind. He ordered his men to retreat. Though Garnett was known as a gallant and courageous general, Stonewall Jackson was infuriated that he retreated, and had him court- martialed for cowardice and unauthorized retreat.

Garnett was a man of honor whose reputation for integrity was important to him, and he was deeply hurt by this accusation.

General Robert E. Lee reassigned him to active duty, and on July 3, 1863 he found himself in a situation similar to that at Kernstown, at Gettysburg. The Union forces were at the top of a hill with cannon and sharpshooters covering a wide open field when General Lee ordered that the Confederates take the hill.

General Longstreet, the second in command under General Lee, protested that it would be physically impossible to take that hill, that the rebel troops would be decimated and would not only lose that battle, but would likely lose the war because of the great loss of men. But Lee thought that the cause was so great, the will of the men so strong, that they could take the hill and win the battle. Though General Longstreet protested the order, he obeyed it and ordered the men to charge, but also ordered that none of the officers ride their horses across the field. To do so would be suicide. Riders would be recognized as officers and would be picked off by cannon fire and rifle fire.

The officers agreed, with one exception. General Garnett mounted his black war horse, "Red Eye" and charged across the open field. His charge was like the "Charge of the Light Brigade," described by Alfred Lord Tennyson's famous poem about the Crimean War. Here is part of the poem: describing the courage of soldiers involved in bloody conflict

> Cannon to right of them,
> Cannon to left of them,
> Cannon in front of them
> Volley'd & thunder'd;
> Storm'd at with shot and shell,
> Boldly they rode and well,
> Into the jaws of Death,
> Into the mouth of Hell.

Richard Garnett was the first general to die at Gettysburg. All the other officers attacked on foot.

Why talk about General Garnett? Because he needed to prove his courage to his men, so that they would know that **he was one of *us*,** a soldier with courage, valor, and honor.

Many soldiers give their lives in the cause of freedom. They do it for love, for integrity, and for *us*. Jesus said it this way, "There is no greater love than that a man lay down his life for his friends." To do this is the ultimate proof that they are one of *us*.

The Only Thing Worth Dying For

I just finished reading a book called "The Only Thing Worth Dying For," by Eric Blehm. It is about the first American men, Green Berets, who died in Afghanistan after the events of what we refer to as 9-11. The book raises the important question, "What is it that is worth dying for?" His answer is that we need to be true to our most noble ideals. That is what is worth dying for.

My question is a similar one: *What is it that is worth living for?* The answer is much the same. The problem is that we need to discover what our most noble ideals are. For most religions, the ideal is love. The problem is that it is natural to love only those we think of as us, and to not love those we think of as *them*.

Chapter Nine
Us Against Them

The tendency to view someone who is different as *them* and someone who is similar as *us* is part of our instinct for *self* preservation. We want to be with people who dress like us, act like us, think like us. Sometimes we will view anyone with a different opinion than ours as *them*. That is why the Catholic Church put *Robin Hood* on its list of forbidden books.

Maybe you didn't know it, but the Catholic Church made up a list of forbidden books that no Catholic was allowed to read. Personally, I don't think it was a good idea for them to do that. Most of the people I knew were more interested in reading those books than the ones that were allowed. They figured the forbidden ones would be more exciting.

I don't think they have a list like that any more, but I'm not sure. You might run across a book someday that has "*Imprimatur*" stamped on the front, meaning this book is one that you are allowed to read if you are a Catholic. It is a book approved by a bishop or somebody who decided it fit into Catholic teaching.

Robin Hood

When the Catholic bishop rode through Sherwood Forest, he would have chests filled with gold and jewels that Robin Hood would take from him and give to the poor. This made the poor people think that Robin was one of *us* and the bishop was one of *them*, because the bishop would not share with the poor, but Robin would.

That is why the book about Robin Hood was on the forbidden list: The Church wanted people to see the bishop and the Church as *us*, and Robin Hood as an outlaw and one of *them*. But the person who told the story of Robin Hood was writing to show that the Church was on the wrong track. Bishops were not supposed to be taking money from the poor and becoming rich; they were supposed to help the poor.

Have you ever played chess? Why do you suppose the bishop in that game is so much more powerful than the pawn? It is because the bishop truly did have power, as one of the wealthy.

The writer of the story of Robin Hood was doing the same thing that Jesus did when he confronted the powerful leaders of the church (synagogue) of his own day, and what Martin Luther did when he confronted the pope and the bishops of his day. They were calling the church to its mission of love. And that is why they all were persecuted by the religious leaders of their day.

Since the time of Constantine it has been important for the church to decide who are *us* and who are *them*. Actually, it is part of human nature to divide the world up that way. But that can lead to war. Even when it doesn't lead to war, it still can hurt others.

Catholics Against Lutherans

I grew up in the Roman Catholic Church and fell in love when I was 20 years old, the age you are now. The problem is that Gail was a Lutheran, and she wanted us to get married in a Lutheran Church. But the pastor of my parish told my family that if I married a Lutheran outside of the Roman Catholic Church I would go to Hell, because only a Roman Catholic priest could validly administer the sacrament of Holy Matrimony for a person baptized as a Catholic. I would be living in sin, and would be excommunicated from the Catholic Church – meaning I could not receive the sacrament of Holy Communion! He told my mom and dad that they should do everything they could to stop our wedding in the Lutheran Church! That was a time for me that was just like you said: "The Church can cause as much harm as good." It also convinced me that I didn't want to raise our children in a church that was so judgmental. So we married in the Lutheran Church.

Traitor!

Here is what I learned from that situation. My intention was to extend or expand who I included as *us*. I wanted to include Lutherans as *us*. After all, we were the same religion, just different denominations. And I had grown to know and love Gail. She was just like *us* except

46

that she was Lutheran. But when I married her, the Catholic Church didn't see it that way. **They thought I had left *us* to join *them***. Anyone outside the Catholic Church was *them*, not *us*.

I learned that whenever you try to include *them* as part of *us*, then people who have been part of us will very likely see you as a **traitor**. They will think you have left *us* to join *them*.

That is a huge problem that stops us from including more people as *us*. We will look at examples in the next chapter, but you probably can think of examples in your own life, how if you are friends with certain people then others will view you as one of *them*.

Fortunately, things change. Catholics and Lutherans now can marry each other with the blessings of the church. Black people can marry white people, something that in President Lincoln's day was illegal and unheard of. But things haven't changed as much as they could, or as much as they will.

Part of the change has been influenced by a man who was a friend of mine, one of the great blessings of my life. His name was Bishop James P. Shannon. I wish you could have known him. He died when you were in high school.

Bishop Shannon

I first met him when I was a senior in high school and he was the President of St. Thomas College. I had won a national award for Junior Achievement, which was an organization to teach high school students about American business. I was named the National Sales Manager of the Year for 1959, and was asked to speak at a banquet attended by a lot of the business leaders in the Twin Cities of Minneapolis and St. Paul. Bishop Shannon then was called Father Shannon (also called Dr. Shannon), because he hadn't been named a bishop yet. He was asked to give the invocation and the benediction for the banquet, and so he and I sat next to each other at the head table.

After my talk, he offered me a scholarship to St. Thomas College, and we talked a lot during the years I was there. I also became his assistant when he said mass. He said mass every day at 7:00 o'clock in the morning, and I would be his altar boy. Sometimes we would spend some time together after the mass. He became my hero. But about the time I married Gail, he was relieved of being a bishop and a pastor in the Catholic Church because he disagreed with the pope about birth control.

He believed that sex could be part of a relationship between a husband and wife even when they did not want or could not afford more children, and he had begun to share this belief with Catholic married couples who came to him for confession or for advice. He told them that if their conscience led them to choose birth control, then they should follow their conscience.

This advice went against "Natural Law," a Catholic doctrine stating that it is a perversion to use sex for anything but procreation. His advice also went against the dictates of the pope. So for following his conscience instead of the word of the pope, he was excommunicated.

He was one of the most Christ-like men I have ever known, featured on the cover of Time magazine and loved by many, but his confrontation with the Church led to his becoming one of *them*.

An Abomination?

This year a friend of mine was told that she was an abomination to God because she was bisexual. She is a wonderful person of great compassion and courage, but feels the pain of that condemnation, of feeling no longer accepted by her church family because of her sexual orientation. One person told her, "I love you even though to God you are an abomination." She didn't feel loved, however, despite those 'loving' words.

She is an inspiration to me. For several years, since the war in Iraq and then Afghanistan, there have been two groups in Anacortes. One group stands on a corner every Sunday with signs that say, "Support our troops! Support the war!" That corner also used to have signs that said, "Support our president." That was when George Bush was president.

On the other corner stood a different group with signs that said, "End the war. Bring our troops home." I think one corner was mostly Republicans, and the other corner mostly Democrats. Ordinarily those two groups displayed animosity toward each other.

But Anna, whose father had twice been deployed with the Navy, would stand one Sunday with one corner, and the next Sunday with the other corner. She viewed both groups as supporting her father, supporting our country.

I wish there were more people like her.

Another gay friend of mine

is a nurse who, when she discovered that a woman she had never met needed a kidney transplant, gave one of her kidneys. "I had two of them, and she needed one of them."

It is not right that she is not given the same welcome in society that other people have. She and her partner had a commitment ceremony, but they are not legally allowed to call themselves married in Washington State.

These are examples that only touch the tip of the iceberg, as they say. Suspicion and even hatred towards Muslims create an atmosphere of hate rather than love, and America is not showing much of a welcome for the Mexicans who want to enter our country. One man put it this way: "I am not prejudiced, and I don't hate black people or Mexicans or even homosexuals. I just want to live and worship with people who think the same as I do." For him, diversity is not a good thing. If people are different from *us*, then they are one of *them*.

We often are against *them* in order to prove that we are one of *us*. We do that because it is too scary to not be included as *us*. This is not only a problem for religion, but for all human beings.

Chapter Ten
We Are Against Them in order to be Part of Us

It's a natural behavior to divide the world into *us* and *them* and to trust and love *us* but to be suspicious of *them*. Often we go to war against *them*, and during the war we hate them and kill them. We call them Japs and Nazis, and Vietnamese Gooks, and other words that make them not even seem like people. The reason we depersonalize them is that if we think of them as people, we are likely, at least on some level, to think of them as one of *us*.

Whether you hate war or whether you like war, we will have war. It is a constant part of our history. As Americans we revolted against the English soldiers who occupied our land and who exacted taxes on our tea and other things. This led to the Boston Tea Party and led *us* to become coffee drinkers -- helping establish our identity as different from the English tea drinkers, an identity proudly maintained now on many street corners by Starbucks. You probably studied the Boston Tea Party in one of your American History classes.

After we won the Revolutionary War we killed the Indians as we claimed all of their land for ourselves and for God, following the example of Joshua when he killed the Canaanites and claimed their land for God and for the Israelites.

But war is a horrible thing. During war we do terrible things, and so does our enemy. Sometimes we do these awful things just to be part of *us*. A person might enlist in war to show everyone that he is one of us, one who will fight for us. "I am not one of them, I am one of us."

This is brought out in a book written by a PLU professor. It is called *ORDINARY MEN: Reserve Police Battalion 101 and the Final Solution in Poland*, and it is written by Christopher Browning. It tells how ordinary men, like the men in our own neighborhood, will give up their integrity in order to be one of us.

I don't know how much you know about World War II. You may not be aware that Germany during the war was a Christian country.

On the belt buckles of the German soldiers the phrase: "Gott Mit Uns," proudly proclaimed "God (is) With Us." But what happened was not very loving or anything God would have approved:

Ordinary Men

The men Dr. Browning writes about were not S.S. (the Nazis known to have committed the greatest atrocities), were not even part of the regular German army during World War II. Many of them had been taught that Jews were evil, but they seldom had any personal contact with Jews. They were ordinary citizens, members of a reserve Nazi police battalion. They were similar to what we call our National Guard. These Germans, part of the Reserve Police Battalion 101, were called from their ordinary lives to travel to Poland and to kill all the Jews in the area they were assigned. They were told that all Jews were the enemy, were not one of *us*, but were *them*.

They were told to march all the Jews including not only the men, but also the women, the infants in their arms, and other children to a remote forest area. They would make them lie down, and then they would put a bullet through the back of their heads.

They were told by their superior officer that because this would be a particularly tough assignment, not for cowards, there would be no punishment if someone decided not to participate. You would think that all of the men would say, "OK, then I'm going home to my wife and family. It makes me sick to even think that anyone would do these terrible things, and I sure am not going to."

But the amazing thing is, almost all of the men participated. They did not want to let down their comrades. They wanted to be one of the group, one of us regardless what they had to do, regardless how horrible the action seemed. One man hesitates. He does not want to kill children. So his partner solves the problem: **The hesitant man can kill the parents, and the partner will then kill the orphaned children** who would not have much of a life in a country occupied by the Nazis. They would be better off dead.

So they find a way, regardless how repugnant, regardless how horrible, to be part of the group, part of *us* instead of siding with or protecting *them*. Why?

Because to refuse to kill might be interpreted that you were in some way a part of *them*, a "Jew lover" and therefore no longer one of *us*. This could lead to disastrous results, not only for the man who refused, but also for his family. To be one of us in this situation is a matter of self preservation.

That is why excommunication and shunning are powerful weapons. "You are no longer one of us. Do not expect us to support you any more." That was the most painful part of my life, being excommunicated from not only the Catholic Church, but from the support of my parents and many Catholic friends. (Though my brother Tom and sisters Carol and Cindy were supportive of what I did by marrying Gail in the Lutheran Church.)

Divorce is painful for the same reason: You are no longer part of *us*. And as we have seen, being one of us can be of vital importance.

So, one very important answer to the question *Why do people go to war and do terrible things* is this: We need to be one of *us*, at almost any cost, and we will do almost anything to prove that we are one of *us*, that we are willing to fight and even to die to protect *us*.

But I want to tell you a story that has had an impact on me. It is about a neighbor of ours when we lived in West Seattle. He was also a member of the church where I was the pastor, and he demonstrates a value in no longer being against *them*. For me, his example is of one who found and then lived his most noble ideals.

Richard's Healing Hands

He was a construction worker, often at the controls of heavy equipment —bulldozers, graders, earth movers. He was tough, a man's man. He had fought in World War II against the Japanese on islands where the fighting was close, where you shot people and they shot at you. Many of his friends were killed on those islands. When the war was over, he hated "Japs."

But after several years went by, he had a strong inclination to visit Hiroshima and Nagasaki, the two cities where America had dropped the atomic bomb. The cities were being rebuilt, but the devastation was terrible. He began to feel the horror of war in a new way. He began to study the Japanese, and in his garden at home he grew bonsai plants and even bought a statue of Buddha to put in what was becoming a Japanese garden.

Then one day he began to cry as he thought of the hundreds of thousands of innocent people killed by the atomic bomb. Later he was surprised to discover that he no longer hated the Japanese.

His wife suffered from arthritis. But as he held her hand when he came in from the garden one day he noticed, and so did she, a warmth coming from his hand. And after the warmth she suddenly exclaimed, "I don't hurt any more! What did you do?" He had done nothing, but during the next several months he had the experience of touching people and then having them ask the same thing: "What did you do?" People in pain began coming to him, asking him to touch them. And many of them left without pain.

I asked him about this because his wife and his wife's sister had talked to me about it. He said that he didn't know what was happening, but somehow he thought it was related to the change in him when he stopped hating the Japanese, and began to think of them as one of *us*, human beings that wanted to live like we do, caring for their children, going shopping with a neighbor, wanting to live a peaceful life.

He died a few years later of something that went wrong with a surgery on a carotid artery in his neck. But when I was in his presence during those years, I sensed peace.

I can't say I know what happened, but I believe that something very intense happened to him when he changed from hate to love, from considering the enemy as *them* to viewing them as one of *us*. I think it has to do with the power of re-membering, and I believe love is at the essence of that power.

We have been in Fallbrook for over two weeks now. We are at the edge of Camp Pendleton, a Marine Corps training facility. Helicopters fly over Julie's house on training missions, and we hear artillery and machine guns as Marines practice with live ammunition. Two young men from Anacortes, Kyle and Tanner, are being trained there, and one of them will soon be deployed to Afghanistan. I love both of those people and their families. They are patriots who love their country. I wish they didn't have to go to war and put their lives in harm's way. But even if I don't like it, war is a fact, and there will always be people who will volunteer to fight for their country.

I hope you never have to kill anybody, but if anyone tried to kill you, I would kill them if that was the only way to protect you. I guess that is one of the ways that the instinct for self preservation overcomes my religious teaching that I should love my enemy. I hope and pray that I will never be in that situation.

Chapter Eleven
We Need an Invitation to Live

Nicole, one of the reasons I told you the stories about Kyle -- about the snail, and about Chair being all the numbers beyond infinity -- is because when Kyle said those things to me he might not have known it, but he was giving me an invitation to live. Love does that, it invites people to live, letting them know that they make someone's life better. Right now, by letting you know that I love you *Chair*, I am hoping you will feel it as a strong invitation to live, and to live fully, exuberantly, and enthusiastically. It tells you that you are important to me because you are one of the reasons I want to stay alive, to benefit from what you give to me just by being yourself.

One of the reasons this is so important is that sometimes people do not know how valuable they are. Right now as I write this to you, a friend of mine is missing. He has been gone for eight days. He was a school counselor at Anacortes High School, and was a kind, gentle man. But when his daughter died, he became depressed and unable to see how important he is to so many people. Now on the Anacortes City website there are many, many people who are writing telling him how important he was (is) to them. Most of them are former students who say he had such an impact on their lives, even that he saved their lives by how he helped them when they were in "darkness." One said, "Your office was so safe, and you were so kind. I knew you cared."

But now he is missing, and people think he may have had an accident, been murdered, or even killed himself. His name is Dr. Keith Anderson, and I hope he turns up alive. I wish I had told him how important he is to me and to so many people. It might have helped him get through the terrible pain of his daughter's death.

We need that affirmation from other people, and you are very good at giving it. You invite me to live all the time just by the ways you let me know that you love me, and you do it for a lot of people. I wish they would all tell you how wonderful that is, and how wonderful you are, because a person needs to know how loved they are, how needed they are.

The Trip to the Emergency Room

Last year you came to visit us in Anacortes just after you moved into the house you are living in at school. I was out in the yard at the edge of the bank that leads down to the water, and I was planting seeds from a Madronna tree, trying to establish new trees so that the bank would not erode during a rainstorm. I slipped and as I was falling down the steep side of the cliff I grabbed onto a branch to stop my fall. I got a sliver that went deep into my hand, as well as some bruises. The sliver was so deep that we couldn't get it out. It broke off, leaving about two inches. When I decided to go to the emergency room to have the doctor remove it, you said, "Grandpa, I'll come and keep you company." It was so unexpected, that you, who I had seen for so long as a little girl, were now taking care of me! And it was so obvious how much you loved me as they gave me a tetanus shot, took x-rays, and cut open my hand so they could remove the sliver. It was in some ways a little thing, but I will always remember you being there in case I needed you. That was a great invitation to live. "I'll drive you home," you said when they had bandaged me up and we were walking out to the car.

Even a Dog can Invite Us to Live

It is a bit surprising, but even dogs can give us an invitation to live. Jordy does that for you; Zoe and Josie do it for me, Greta and Lola do it for Julie. When we have been gone for a while and then come home, their wagging tails and excited jumping around says, "I'm so glad you are finally home! I have missed you so much!" It's a sign of love, and it's an invitation to live. We are appreciated, needed. For them, we are one of *us*. I have heard that a person will live longer if they do not live alone, that even a dog or cat can add years to their lives. Part of the reason is that it gives them a reason to live, to take care of the animal. But I think a stronger reason is that the animal invites them to live, just by loving them. The animal is somehow saying, "You are one of *us*, one of my family, I need you and I love you.

PART THREE: JESUS

Chapter Twelve
Hope, Light, and Love

I think it is amazing that a small group of Christians living in the Roman Empire over two thousand years ago became billions of people who influenced the whole world. There are several reasons why this happened. I want to mention two of the main ones

One reason for the rapid spread of Christianity is that it offers hope. All of us at some times experience what we might call darkness. And Jesus offered hope -- a light for the darkness. At first this appealed mainly to the poorer people of the Roman Empire, those who were slaves or who worked hard with little pay or who suffered from severe illness. The Bible predicted that for those who lived in darkness the light would come and the light would shine not only in the darkness, but in us. Here is how Emily understood it:

Emily

When Emily was three years old (but she would say "I'm three and a half!") she went to a Sunday school class and learned a song called *This little light of mine.* The song had several verses and even hand motions. She would hold up her hand with one finger pointing at the sky and sing, "This little light of mine, I'm goin' to let it shine." Another verse would be "All around the neighborhood, I'm goin' to let it shine." One of the verses was "Hide it under a bushel? No! I'm goin' to let it shine, let it shine, let it shine."

Well, Emily didn't know what a bushel was. But she knew what a bush was. So she sang that verse like this: "Hide it under a bush? Hell no! I'm goin' to let it shine, let it shine, let it shine."

I think this is a funny story, but like all stories it has wisdom. You have a light and you let it shine. But sometimes it takes a lot of determination not to let it get put out. "Hide it under a bush? Hell No! I'm goin' to let it shine!" Sometimes we have to say "No!" to the forces of hell and darkness and just let our light shine. So Emily found a meaning that is important.

But here is a story of a man whose light had pretty much gone out, until he saw Jesus as a light for him:

Tom

We will call him Tom. He was a dairy farmer who liked to fly. He had his own plane and a pilot's license, and he would fly over his dairy farm and over large areas of California, just for fun. But one day his plane crashed. "It was pilot error," he told me. "I don't remember for sure just what went wrong, but I think it had to do with a downdraft, a wind coming down the side of a mountain." Anyway, he crashed and almost died. They took him to the nearest hospital, which was a Catholic hospital. He was Lutheran.

He told me that when he woke up three or four days after the crash, they had amputated one leg, and he was in pain all over, somewhat delirious with the pain and the painkilling medication. He felt that his life was over.

But when he opened his eyes, he saw on the wall a crucifix, a cross with the figure of Jesus still nailed to it. Most Lutheran churches have an empty cross that symbolizes the resurrection, but Catholics often have the crucifix with the figure of the dying Jesus.

"When I saw that cross, I thought of the suffering that Jesus went through for me. I thought that if he could suffer and die for me, then I could stand the pain I was going through. Jesus was with me in that room and that gave me the strength to go on."

Now he still has some pain from the artificial leg they gave him (the artificial leg is called a *prosthesis*.) But he does well and is now an inspiration for others who have pain, especially those who have to have a limb removed. Jesus was his light, but now he has become a light for others.

I have known alcoholics who told me that they never could have shaken that addiction except that they believed Jesus was there for them to find a way out. And I remember being in a hospital waiting room.

Elizabeth

We will call her Elizabeth. I knew her when I was a student pastor, something like a student teacher, learning how to be a professional.

I remember one day in a hospital waiting room where I was waiting with her husband while she was having surgery for cancer. Finally a doctor came out and told us that she was filled with cancer, so much that they didn't even try to remove it. He cautioned us that she did not have much hope for more than a few months of life.

But when I, as her pastor, went into the recovery room to have a prayer with her, she told me, "Don't worry! I am going to be ok. Jesus came to me and assured me that I will get well."

I thought she probably had a hallucination caused by the drugs they had given her. But six months later she cooked a dinner for all the guests that came for her son's confirmation. And she was healthy! I was still receiving Christmas letters from her many years later, until we lost contact when we moved to Everett. As far as I know, she is still healthy. Jesus brought her hope, and healing. And that apparently was the experience of early Christians and was a reason for the spread of Christianity. People need hope.

A second reason Christianity spread so quickly is that the focus of the life and the teachings of Jesus is love. This is so important it needs to be emphasized over and over again. Love is the heart of Christianity, summarized in just a few words by St. John. Love is what helps us expand our world to the size of the ocean instead of just our own little well. Without love, life loses its meaning. The story of the Good Samaritan is a story of love, not just for those who are *us*, but also for *them*. And that is what we will look at next.

Chapter Thirteen
Jesus and the Good Samaritan

The most important idea I have ever heard is that love is the purpose of life. But too many people make it into a multiple choice test:

Is the purpose in life (A) To gain power or make as much money as possible; (B) To pleasure our bodies with food, drink, sex, and whatever makes us feel good; (C) To study and obtain knowledge; or (D) To love and have compassion for all human life.

For Jesus and for the followers or disciples of Jesus, the answer is obvious and indisputable. We have choices to make, and the choice to love and have compassion for all human life is the only right response not only to a written test, but to all of the situations in which we find ourselves.

The early disciples knew that we are called to love *all* human beings, not just family or those who are like us or live near us. Jesus made that very clear when a lawyer approached him and asked, "Teacher, what must we do to be saved?" Another way to ask this question is "What must we do to have the best possible life?" Jesus replied, "What does the law say?" The lawyer answered correctly that the law tells us to love God with our whole heart, mind, and soul, and to love our neighbor as ourselves. Jesus told him he was correct, to do that and live. The lawyer replied, "But who is my neighbor?"

Then, to clarify who our neighbor is, Jesus told the story of the Good Samaritan. But before we look at that story, it is a good idea to give some background about who the Samaritans were.

They were originally Jews. But twice in their history before the birth of Jesus, the Jews were defeated in war and many were taken into captivity. They were determined to keep their own identity, especially their worship of the One True God.

However, as the years went by many of them began to merge with the culture of those who had captured them. Some of them married foreign women and allowed the worship of the foreign gods, erecting idols even in their own household. This was considered to be an abomination by those who stayed true to their own beliefs.

It would have been something like when the Nazis occupied much of Europe. Some of the French or other nationalities became collaborators with their captors, much to the disgust of the underground and those who saw the Nazis as evil, as enemy. When the war was over, those who joined with the Nazis were punished by those who fought against the Germans.

That's the way it was for many of the Jews. When they were finally freed (the Persians, led by Cyrus, defeated the Babylonians and issued an edict that all the Jews could go home) they went home, but they would not let the collaborators live with them in Israel or Judah. The collaborators established an area known in the Bible as Samaria. This whole area was considered to be unclean by the rest of the Jews. If they were to travel from the Northern Kingdom of Israel to the Southern Kingdom of Judah, they had to take a major detour around Samaria, which was centered between those two places where the Jews lived.

Jesus, however, travelled through Samaria and even talked with a Samaritan woman at a well in Samaria. Not only was she a Samaritan, she also was an adulteress who had lived with five men who were not her husband. She was not only considered unclean as a Samaritan, but she was an abomination to God because she was an adulteress. The penalty for her actions was to be stoned to death. But Jesus talked casually with her and she brought others to see this prophet among them.

So when the lawyer asked Jesus, "But who is my neighbor?" it was a scandal to hear how he answered.

The Good Samaritan

Jesus told a story about a man who was walking from Jerusalem to Jericho and robbers beat him, took what he had, and left him lying beside the road. A Priest of the Jews passed by him. Then a Levite, another religious leader of the Jews, passed by him. Finally a Samaritan took pity on the wounded man. He poured oil on his wounds, put him on his donkey and took him to an inn where he said to the innkeeper that he would pay any expenses incurred by this man as he recovered.

Jesus then asked the lawyer, "Which one of these was a neighbor to the wounded man?" And the answer was obvious: The Samaritan.

If Jesus had lived during the time when Joshua was killing the Canaanites, he would have told the story about *the Good Canaanite*. If he lived during the Crusades against the Jews and Muslims, he would have told the story about *The Good Jew* or *the Good Muslim*. If he lived during the Civil Rights struggles he would have told the story about *The Good African American*. Now it would be the story of *The Good Homosexual*.

The reason this story is so important is that it makes clear that our neighbor is not just someone we regard as one of *us*. It can even be someone who is a traitor to us, a collaborator with the enemy, or even a heretic, one who has forsaken our God.

Though that is a core teaching of Jesus, it is not easy to follow.

For just one example, read the fourth chapter of the Gospel of Luke. Jesus tells people in a synagogue at Nazareth that God loves people who are not Jews, and he gives the example of a widow in a foreign country who was saved from starvation by the prophet Elijah and a leper healed by the prophet Elisha even though the leper was an army officer of a country that was viewed as an enemy. The Bible says,

When they heard this, all in the synagogue were filled with rage. They got up, drove him out of the town, and led him to the brow of the hill on which their town was built, so that they might hurl him off the cliff."

They were enraged at the implication that God loved *them* as much as *us*. In fact, they wanted to kill Jesus for implying that they were not the only chosen people of God, that God loved others also.

Jesus taught that the most important thing in the world is love, and that we should love all human life as created in God's own image. This teaching changed the lives of many who heard it. Stories are told of Christians going to their death, thrown to the wild animals in the Coliseum, singing hymns. They did not seem to act in hatred even toward their worst enemies.

But since the time of Constantine things changed. That is why a man named Michael Hart does not rate Jesus as the most influential person in history.

Chapter Fourteen
Jesus is Number Three

Michael Hart in his book *The 100: A Ranking of the Most Influential Persons in History*, ranks Jesus as the world's third most influential person in history, trailing Muhammad and Sir Isaac Newton and followed by Buddha, Confucius, and St. Paul. The reason Jesus was not listed as number one? People generally do not live up to the teachings of Jesus.

He does not dispute that Jesus may have been the most holy person in the history of the world, or that he was the Son of God, or that he could walk on water or even raise people from the dead. He is only interested in how much influence Jesus has had on the history of the world compared to Muhammad and others. Walking on water or raising the dead, for instance, is spectacular but unless the behavior of his followers is influenced by his actions, it does not count for Mr. Hart. He explains as follows, beginning with a quote from the King James Version of the Bible. Jesus states:

Ye have heard that it hath been said, Thou shalt love thy neighbor, and hate thine enemy. But I say unto you, Love your enemies, bless them that curse you, do good to them that hate you, and pray for them which despitefully use you, and persecute you.

Michael Hart comments:

Now, these ideas – which were not a part of the Judaism of Jesus' day, nor of most other religions – are surely among the most remarkable and original ethical ideas ever presented. If they were widely followed, I would have had no hesitation in placing Jesus first in this book.

But the truth is that they are not widely followed. In fact, they are not even generally accepted. Most Christians consider the injunction to "Love your enemy" as – at most—an ideal which might be realized in some perfect world, but one which is not a reasonable guide to conduct in the actual world we live in. We do not normally practice it, do not expect others to practice it, and do not teach our children to practice it. Jesus' most distinctive teaching, therefore, remains an intriguing but basically untried suggestion. (pp 20-21)

There is convincing evidence that for the first approximately 300 years after the death of Christ those who followed Jesus were very influenced by him, inspired by his life and his teachings. Their lives were radically transformed, so much so that they felt reborn and some, like St. Paul, even changed their names (from Saul to Paul, for instance) to indicate their new life. They prayed for their enemies, loved one another, and submitted with prayers or hymns on their lips as Roman soldiers threw them to the animals in the coliseum. They sacrificed their own lives rather than to take the life of another, influenced by the example and teachings of their Lord. They began to view their neighbor as being anyone and everyone. Their changed lives so inspired the Western World that the birth of Christ became the dividing line between two separate epochs known as B.C. (before Christ) and A.D. (*anno domino*, meaning "in the year of our Lord. If only these first years were to be evaluated by Michael Hart, he would have listed Jesus as the world's most influential person.

But since the time of Constantine many Christians have done just as Michael Hart has indicated. They have decided not to take seriously the injunction to "Love your enemy," and have acted in accordance with their instinct for *self* preservation. So, what happened?

PART FOUR: CHRISTIANS ENTER THE WHITE HAT – BLACK HAT WAR

.

Chapter Fifteen
Constantine's Legacy

Humans have always found ways to turn good into evil, blessings into curses. We are able to pervert, misuse, abuse, distort and exploit not only the Bible but almost every good thing. Primitive peoples used fire to warm their caves and homes, to cook their food, and to bring light into the darkness where wild animals prowled just beyond the campfire. Fire was a wonderful discovery, a great blessing. But it didn't take long before it was used to burn down the shelters or teepees of people who were viewed as *them*, as *not us*; as enemies. Christians who lit candles during their worship services also learned to use fire to burn heretics at the stake.

Throughout history almost every blessing has also been used for evil. Nuclear energy, a force so powerful that it could provide electric power for all the cities of the world, has been used to destroy entire cities – killing, maiming, bringing lingering but deadly radiation sickness and death to those who survived the blast. Biology and chemistry have provided not only vaccines and medicines for healing, but are helping stockpile chemical and biological weapons of mass destruction able to kill most or even all of humankind.

Even the power of sex -- a blessing able to bring about new life, making us co-creators with God – has been misused, and religion has been very much a part of its *mis*use, and its *ab*use, teaching on the one hand that sex is a gift from God to unite a man and woman in a way that brings about a family; but teaching also that sex is sinful and therefore forbidden to those who want to lead a devout life in the priesthood or as a nun.

There are almost endless examples, all demonstrating the same thing: It is not only fire, nuclear power, biology, chemistry and sex, but all forms of power that we can, and do, misuse – including religion, Since the time of Constantine even Christianity has been misused.

When Constantine was a general in the Roman Army he claimed to have seen a vision of a cross (or possibly it was the Chi Rho, the first two Greek letters in the word "Christ") in the clouds and the words, *In Hoc Signo vinces*, "In this sign you will conquer." So the sign of the cross, at first a spear with a crossbar and later an insignia on the shields of his soldiers, led his army into battle. Or, according to some accounts Constantine ordered that the soldiers paint a cross on their shields. But however they did it, in that sign Constantine did conquer, proving that God was on his side. Christianity now became the official religion of the Roman Empire. Constantine then changed the name of the empire to The *Holy* Roman Empire.

It was a good political move for Constantine. Many Romans had been impressed with the early Christians and were becoming disgusted with Roman morality. They would watch as Christians, including pregnant women and children, often praying or singing hymns, were thrown to the animals in the coliseum. The Roman ideals of honor and nobility were being transgressed by these bloody spectacles. So Constantine gained favor with the people when he decided the whole empire would now be Christian.

The problem was that he didn't really know what Christianity was about, because up until that time he had worshipped the Roman gods. So in 325 A.D. he gathered the Christian bishops together at Nicea to write down what Christians believed. *Nicea* is a Latinized version (the Romans at the time of Constantine spoke Latin, a Roman language) of the Greek word "Nike," which means "victory." If you wear Nike shoes, for instance, you are wearing shoes of victory. *If your name is Nicole, you are named for victory!*

The town where the bishops met was named Nicea in order to celebrate Constantine's victories. Their statement of faith became known as the Nicene Creed, or the "creed of victory," a celebration of Constantine's conquest. The Nicene Creed became part of the Orthodox belief of the Christian Church.

Once this statement of faith, the Nicene Creed, was available, Constantine used his power to convert all of the people in the Holy Roman Empire to Christianity, uniting the Empire and eliminating any enemies who refused to honor him as absolute ruler.

Constantine was a military man, and he organized the Christian Church in the same pattern as the military. It was a chain of command. The pope and the emperor were at the head. You obeyed them. The bishops were in charge of a district, and you obeyed them. The priests were in charge of a parish, and you obeyed them.

Christianity was now the state religion, bringing the *pax Romana* to the entire Western World. But those who were not *us* were *them*, and it was always us against them. Now it was the Christians, the true believers, against *them,* those who did not accept the Nicene Creed.

Constantine and Orthodoxy

For some religious people, and this is especially true for patriarchal religions that view God as the One True God who has chosen only *us* as His Chosen People, the conflict between us and them is intensified by an emphasis on orthodoxy. The word comes from the Greek words *ortho*, (right, straight, true) and *doxy* (teaching.) An orthodontist is one who makes teeth *(dent)* straight, or right, or true. Orthodoxy means "right or true teaching."

Orthodoxy is what helps people decide who is *us* and who is *them*. If you don't believe what I believe, then you are one of them. I have the right teaching; my church is the One True Faith. If you are not one of *us*, then God is not with you, because you are not one of God's people.

The problem is that the "right teaching" is only one interpretation of the Bible. People have interpreted the Bible to support almost anything.

Orthodoxy and the Bible

If it's written in the Bible, then it is what we believe. It is what is orthodox. It is the Word of God. If we can get the Bible (or the Quran or any other Holy Scripture) to support us, we can then view ourselves as the righteous ones, and we can claim that God is on our side. So we interpret the Bible to support our viewpoint:

For instance,

Ole and Lena were still in bed one morning when Lena said, "Ole, how about you get up and make coffee this morning?"

Ole replied, "I would, but you know Lena, that making coffee and doing the cooking are women's work. The kitchen is no place for a man."

Lena: "If I can show you in the Bible that it's the man's job to make the coffee, would you do it then?"

Ole, after a pause while he thought about this: "Yes Lena, if it's in the Bible I'll do it. The Bible is the Word of God. That's why a woman is subject to her husband, it's in the Bible. That's why woman is man's companion, it's in the Bible. But I am certain that there is nothing in the Bible about coffee. Yet, if I am wrong, I'll certainly follow the Word of God."

So Lena took her Bible which was on the dresser by the bed, and opened it up, showing Ole a whole chapter titled "He brews."

When Constantine conquered the whole known Western World, he made Christianity the One True Faith, and he then began persecuting all "heretics," the people who did not believe the Nicene Creed, the people who were not *orthodox*.

This is when Christianity became a religion of *us against them*. It helped unify the Roman Empire, but it changed Christianity from a religion of love for all people. The message of Jesus and the message of the story of the Good Samaritan became less important than being one of *us*. That is why Michael Hart rates Jesus as only number three in his list of the most influential people in the world. Since Constantine it has become again a world of *us against them*.

Chapter Sixteen
Ethnic Cleansing

It is part of human nature to go to war and kill the enemy, and Joshua and the Israelites believed that was the right thing to do. The early Christians often followed in the path of Jesus who gave his own life rather than killing anyone else, but since the time of Constantine people have let that instinct take over again. Constantine gave permission for people to trust in war as a way to bring peace, for those with the strongest army to rule the world. And he used religion as a way to unify the Holy Roman Empire. Everyone was now *us*. Or otherwise you were a conquered people, subject to Rome.

From the time of Constantine until now, war has been the method used to bring peace. The conquering of America by the Europeans is one example.

Jared Diamond's Pulitzer Prize winning book *Guns, Germs, and Steel* explains that when the white Europeans came to the new continent that we now call America, they posed a threat to the "Indians." (That label came from their belief that they had landed in India.) They carried with them germs that decimated the people they encountered in the new land. (*Decimate* originally meant killing one out of ten. When one of the Roman Legions lost a battle, one out of ten would be killed as punishment. But later, as in the case of the American Indians, *decimate* meant the loss of nine out of ten people. Sometimes it means everyone has died.)

At first the deaths were unintentional consequences of contact between the different societies, but in some cases blankets filled with Smallpox germs were intentionally introduced into the American Indian society, killing the recipients who had developed no resistance. Warfare became inevitable when the pale Europeans began settling on the land that the Indians used as hunting grounds, killing the bison that the Indians needed for food, clothing, and shelter (the hides would become walls for the teepees). At first there were treaties granting certain rights to the Indians forever, including possession of some of their native lands. But eventually these lands became reservations, and then there was a need for railroads through the reservations, and then gold was found in the Black Hills. This is the way Black Elk understood the situation, as recorded in a book called *Black Elk Speaks:*

Up on the Madison Fork the Wasichus (whites) had found much of the yellow metal that they worship and that makes them crazy, and they wanted to have a road up through our country to the place where the yellow metal was; but my people did not want the road. It would scare the bison and make them go away, and also it would let the other Wasichus come in like a river. They told us that they wanted only to use a little land, as much as a wagon would take between the wheels; but our people knew better. And when you look about you now, you can see what it was they wanted.

When the Indians began resisting the invasion and occupation of the land, their fate was sealed. Sioux and Cheyenne Indians defiantly left their reservations to fight the invaders who were intruding into their sacred lands in the Black Hills. They were met by Lt. Colonel George Custer and the Seventh Cavalry who tried to put down the rebellion of the "Red Devils" who were led by Sitting Bull. It was *us*, who had God on our side, against *them*, the *Red Devils.*

The Indians won, for the last time. Custer's Last Stand at the Little Bighorn River became the last stand for the Indians as well, due to the outrage of the citizens of the United States who wanted revenge for the "murder" or "massacre" of Custer and his men. There was no indication that the Indians were defending themselves from an attack by the cavalry. Indians had become what we might now term the "evil empire."

An Indian friend of mine recalls his grandfather repeating the slogan of the white man:

"The only good Indian is a dead Indian."

The invaders eventually turned most of the Indians into "good" Indians. Much of this behavior was justified by the Christian invaders because the Indians were savages, pagans, and of the devil. They were evil, we were good. Too late, the Indians realized that the Europeans were a deadly threat to them. At the hands of *us* few of *them* survived.

Throughout human history, one group has killed another, often using God as an excuse. God is on our side, against the enemy.

Our next chapter gives a few examples.

Chapter Seventeen
The Ku Klux Klan and Other Perversions of Religion

On Christmas Eve of 1865, at the end of the Civil War and after the death of President Lincoln, six men met in a law office in Pulaski, Tennessee to form a brotherhood which became known as the KKK or Ku Klux Klan. John Lester, James Crowe, John Kennedy, Calvin Jones, Richard Reed, and Frank McCord were the first members of a men's social club patterned after the style of the college fraternities of that day. Originally it was a harmless group that wore funny costumes and saw themselves as a *circle* of friends who would play practical jokes on unsuspecting people. To create an aura of mystery they invented a funny-sounding name: the Ku Klux Klan, taken from the Greek word "*Kuklos*," meaning "circle," or "in a circle." They were a clan, a circle of friends.

Their funny costumes were at first just for fun, but gradually things changed. The costumes began to be masks and a means of intimidation. The group began to view itself as a tribe or a clan organized to protect those Southerners who were downtrodden after the Civil War and who had no militia to protect them. Since the death of Lincoln, with President Andrew Johnson now in charge, the North had become more interested in revenge instead of reconciliation. It was a time of chaos for much of the South after the war, and the KKK was there to protect the Southerners and to enforce what they believed was right.

Two women, in a Bible study group I lead at a retirement home, have talked about their memories of the KKK. They both, one from Arkansas and one from Texas, remember their parents putting on the KKK robes. "It was to warn people who were doing wrong. First they would burn a cross to let them know that they were being warned. If that didn't work, they would burn their barn or finally their house. Sometimes people were hung as an example. It was about the only way to have law and order in those days."

Eventually the clan acted to preserve racial and religious purity during a time when immigrants and other religious denominations were infiltrating the United States, and when slavery had been abolished in the South and the black sharecroppers began acting in ways that were too "uppity" for many in the South. Rosa Parks sitting in the front of the bus is one such example of a black person acting "uppity." For a black man to stare at a white woman was another. To swim at the same beach, to drink from the same water fountain were other acts among many.

The gene pool in America was becoming too diverse for the KKK. Their need for preservation of a pure gene pool emerged as a dominant force, though that may not be the way they described their purpose. They believed that God was on their side, that God was white, and that he wore a white hat. **White was good, black was evil.**

It is not uncommon for the instinct for self-preservation and the desire to pass on our genetic strain to be in conflict with our desire to act with love and compassion for others. The Ku Klux Klan is a stark example of this conflict. The Klan rationalized the use of brute force and intimidation to overpower their rivals whose DNA was different from the "pure white Christian American" DNA. The Klansmen convinced themselves that they were acting out of noble, even religious impulses. They burned a cross during their ceremonies and on the lawns of those they wanted to intimidate. Rather than admit that they were siding with instinct and acting in hatred or fear of those who were different, they claimed the light of the burning cross of Jesus guided them in their actions. They were for Christ, for America and for its flag.

America was their tribe. They used patriotism and religion, not bigotry or instinct, as the explanation for their behavior. The Ku Klux Klan is an example of a tribal religion and *Gott Mit Uns*. They solved the conflict between instinct and religion by claiming that there is no conflict between the two. To dominate, intimidate, or eliminate Jews and blacks and Catholics was not only to be patriotic, but to do the will of God. God is With Us. That's how they rationalized, how they justified their behavior.

They are not alone. There is some of the *us against them* in all of us, even in those we think of as saints.

Saint Olaf

When I taught at St. Olaf College in Northfield Minnesota I was surprised to discover why King Olaf Haraldsson II, who lived from 995 to July 29, 1030 was given the title of *Saint* Olaf. (He is also sometimes referred to as *Rex Perpetuus Norvegiae,* eternal King of Norway.)

In the year 1015 Olaf declared himself King of Norway, and within a few years had annihilated his opposition, and then enforced the acceptance of Christianity throughout Scandinavia, forcing his subjects to be baptized on pain of death. He was canonized as Norway's patron saint only a year after his death, on August 3, 1031. (His canonization was made official by the papal curia in 1888.) He had unified the country, largely through the Christianization of the nation. Now they were all *us.*

The Crusades

In the year 1096 A.D., Pope Urban II as the leader of the Christians had the authority to call for a Holy War against the Muslims. The result was not only death for the Muslims, but also for Jews who were in the way of the Crusaders on their way to the Holy Land with the Cross of Christ sewed on their clothes. Forgetting that the cross was meant to be a symbol of self-sacrifice, they soaked it in the blood of others. Tens of thousands of knights led by Duke Godfrey of Bouillon were joined by thousands of peasants led by Peter the Hermit. Together they spent three years killing every Jew they met on their way to Jerusalem, and in 1099 they "freed" the Holy City from the Infidels by wading in blood up to their ankles, slaughtering every man, woman, and child who was either Muslim or Jew. (This is described in a book by Michael Foss: *People of the First Crusade.* It's one of the books listed in our bibliography.)

One hundred years after the first Crusade, Pope Innocent III said that the Albigensians were heretics, and he sponsored a crusade against them. When seven-thousand people took refuge in the Church of Mary Magdalene and claimed to be Catholics, Arnaud Amalric, the legate in charge of the pope's army ordered them all to be massacred. He knew that there were many Albigensians mixed in with the Catholics, and he didn't want any of them to get away. **"Kill them all," he said. "God will know His own!"**

The reasons the popes called for crusades against Jews and heretics may be varied, but one reason certainly was to gain power for the Catholic Church. Christianity had preached love for all peoples, but at the same time had also claimed that Jesus is the only One Way to salvation. Pope Boniface VIII (1294-1303) went one step further when he made it official: The Roman Catholic Church was the only way to salvation, now identified with the Body of Christ on earth. If you didn't belong to the Roman Catholic Church you would go to Hell. James Carroll, in his book *Constantine's Sword: The Church and the Jews* quotes the Papal Bull issued by Boniface under the title *Unam Sanctam*:

> ...we are obliged to believe and maintain that the Church is one, holy, catholic, and also apostolic. We believe in her firmly and we confer with simplicity that outside of her there is neither salvation nor the remission of sin (P. 315.)

This paved the way for people to be free of guilt when they killed those who had not been baptized into the Catholic Church. If they caused pain and death for some, they might also cause fear in others who would be baptized and then their souls would be saved. Without torture or fear of death they might go to their graves unsaved. So we would be doing them a huge favor if we put the fear of us as well as the fear of God into their souls. In order to save them, of course.

The Inquisition followed the Crusades, and the witchcraft trials followed the Inquisition. In our Century it was the Holocaust.

Hitler

If we are convinced that God is on our side, then whatever we do as *us* is God's will. God is with us. To help us believe that God is on our side, we may select and interpret our Holy Scriptures so that they proclaim that what we believe is the right belief, that our religion is the orthodox one. We are right, and those who do not agree with us are wrong. That is the reason Hitler focused on the scripture that said to obey the governing authorities because they are placed there by God:

Let every person be subject to the governing authorities. For there is no authority except from God, and those that exist have been instituted by God. Therefore he who resists the authorities resists what God has appointed, and those who resist will incur judgment. (Romans 13: 1-2.)

The Bible used in that way helped Hitler convince the German people to accept him as their leader, their *fuehrer*, and he used the Bible to convince them that he should be obeyed. For us, this may seem strange, but the Germans were not that different from us. We are all *us*, and *Gott Mit Uns* lurks in the heart of every human being.

Chapter Eighteen
Homosexuality and Patriarchy

Remember, I am writing as a response to what you said at the restaurant: One reason you thought the Church and the Bible were causing harm is because they are against homosexuals, and you have friends you know are good people who are gay or lesbian. You are right, of course. Any behavior that is not of love is not right, and is not of God.

But human beings have struggled with their fear of strangers probably since they first met those who were different in some way. For many heterosexual people, those who are not heterosexual are different and strange. Some call those who are gay "queer."

Fear of strangers can do terrible things, because the fear can be exaggerated out of control. The Nazis in Germany let that happen, or caused that to happen as the Christians related to Jews as being less than human, and that was an important issue as the Second World War began.

Heterosexuals sometimes blame gay men for spreading AIDS, and for becoming predators who molest young boys. When this happens, they put gay people in a separate category of those to be feared. They forget the predatory actions of heterosexuals toward women in order to blame *them* for sexual sins. They forget the healthy and loving behaviors of many gay people and focus on *us against them.*

The church in Fallbrook that used to be a Lutheran church as part of the ELCA (Evangelical Lutheran Church of America) has left the ELCA because the ELCA recently agreed to allow gay persons to be ordained. They are not the only church that has separated itself from others for similar reasons.

I know of one church that took a vote. The pastor said, "All of you who want to abide by God's Word and the Bible, vote YES, we will leave the ELCA. All of you who do not believe the Bible and who want to go against the Word of *God*, vote NO."

Part of the reason gay and lesbian people are discriminated against is because the Bible discriminates against them. The Hebrew Scriptures (the Old Testament) say that homosexuals are an "abomination" to the Lord, and the Christian Scriptures (the New Testament) indicate that a man who lies with another man as if with a woman is engaging in a perverse behavior. So, let's look at that.

The Bible and the Word of God

It is important to know that the Bible is *not* the unchanging Word of God. The fact is that the Bible changes as it relates to different times and changing societies, even if the printed words remain the same. We change the meaning of the words as our society changes. I'll talk about that in more detail, but I'll give you some examples now. For instance, we no longer sacrifice animals at the altar of our church, even though the Bible says we are to do that. We no longer think the world is the center of the universe, but believe the earth revolves around the sun. We no longer kill people for committing adultery, though the Bible gives that as a punishment. We no longer think that people are committing adultery if they divorce and remarry. We no longer think a woman is cursed by God if she does not produce children. We no longer believe that slaves should obey their masters; in fact we no longer believe slavery is a good idea. And so on.

Jesus gave us the example of how to understand the Bible when he said, "You have heard it said, an eye for an eye and a tooth for a tooth. But I say to you, love your enemies and pray for those who persecute you." He was quoting the Bible, and he changed it. If we follow the example of Jesus, we see that what has been written in the Bible can be changed to make the world more loving, more compassionate. Love your enemies rather than eye for an eye. And that gives us the way to interpret the Bible. It is about love.

As we have already seen, a person wants to be one of *us*. A person who is not gay wants to prove that he is straight, that he is one of *us*. He might resort to cruelty to prove it, like the soldiers who killed Jews or like the gang member who killed the woman in West Seattle just to prove that he would do anything to be one of the gang.

But there is something interesting about this. Hitler, for instance, was part Jew, and he was the one who hated Jews the most. Sometimes people who are part homosexual do the same thing, they are the most vocal about being against *them*. It is very strange, but some of the most condemning preachers against homosexuals turn out to be homosexuals themselves. But they want to be one of *us* so much that they turn against *them*. That way they think nobody will suspect that they too might have homosexual tendencies.

Homosexual people were especially considered to be an abomination in a patriarchal society. In a society where men are in control, they want to be in control of all aspects of society, including sexuality. They do not want women choosing women rather than men as sexual partners; women belong to the men and need to obey them.

Patriarchy also was a society that needed children, many children. So they imposed the death penalty for gay and lesbian people -- people who did not produce children, and who did not act like *us*.

We are learning not to be so prejudiced and so ruled by men, but the prejudice against homosexuals still lingers. If a person is gay or lesbian, many people even today believe that it is their job to convert them to a heterosexual life. They ignore the findings of science that indicate a person is born either gay or straight, and even though behavior can be changed, the tendency to remain gay or to remain straight is influenced by genetics.

The Rainbow Flag

Anacortes is a wonderful place to live. But even in Anacortes there are people who are viewed by some as being different and therefore not one of *us*.

The Congregational church in town often displays a rainbow flag, and they have a sign that says, "Everyone is welcome to worship here." Several times that flag has been taken by vandals, and each time it has been replaced by the congregation – sometimes after a delay of several weeks while they make or buy a new one

You might think that a rainbow flag and a welcoming sign on the church lawn would be taken as a good thing. Everyone is welcome.

But some people view that flag as a threat to marriage, a threat to the literal understanding of the Bible, a sign that the traditional values are disintegrating. For people who have those thoughts, the flag is a threat.

The Hebrew Scriptures and the Christian Scriptures indicate that sexuality is for procreation, and if it is used for any other reason, it is a sin. "Be fruitful and multiply," is the command from God to Adam and Eve, and we are to obey that. (Except for Jesus, and priests and nuns and some other exceptions.) The Roman Catholic Church says that it is part of the "Natural Law" for sex to be used only for procreation. It is natural only for one married couple, one man and one woman to have sex, and to have children.

That is why Bishop Shannon was disciplined when he wrote to the pope that married couples should be able to be sexual even when they did not want or could not afford to have more children. He said they should be allowed to use birth control. According to the pope and Catholic tradition, he was going against "Natural Law" by giving this counsel. But what is natural is not always very civilized, very compassionate, or very "Christian."

Natural Law

A young lion, for example, follows the "Law of Nature," or "Natural Law." As he gains in strength he will challenge the dominant male of a pride, or tribe, who has been hoarding the females for himself. The young lion will not be able to pass on his DNA unless he wins the battle for dominance. When he wins, as he eventually will, a strange thing happens. He will kill the young cubs sired by the old guy. Then he will mate with the females, preserving his own DNA as he destroys the DNA of his rival

Human beings are not entirely different from the lion. We who are members of the same human family are also willing to kill those who are potential threats to us by passing on their genes instead of ours. This is true not only in wars, but is also true in families.

In the not so distant past, if a man had sex with another man's wife, he might be killed by the husband, and the husband could get by without punishment. At least that is part of our human history.

I remember one night when your mother was just a baby and we lived in Northfield Minnesota. Gail and I had been out for the evening and a student from St. Olaf College had been babysitting. I drove her back to the dormitory, and when I got back to our house there was a car parked in the middle of the street. Then police came with sirens blaring. The man in the car had come home to find his wife with a lover, and he had killed both of them out of jealous rage. (He was later found not guilty of murder by reason of temporary insanity.)

Our instinct for *self*-preservation is part of Natural Law, or what comes naturally for us. And this instinct has often led us to fight against *them*. Certainly it was the practice of a patriarchal society, and there was a time when that worked for *us*.

Things have changed however, since the Bible was written, including the laws. Whereas children were once so needed that patriarchy allowed men to have more than one wife in order to produce more children, now we are in a world where overpopulation is the challenge. Children are now not as needed to work the fields or serve in the army, mostly due to mechanized farming and warfare. Infant and maternal deaths have been reduced dramatically. Birth control is now in widespread use, used even by many Catholic couples, despite the Catholic teaching of Natural Law. Our society is changing. Homosexuality was considered to be a threat because it did not produce children, and children were needed. But now the persecution of homosexuality is backed only by prejudice.

PART FIVE: CREATION STORIES

Chapter Nineteen
Coyote, Fox, and Helldiver the Duck

Before Constantine, Christianity was a religion based on the person and teachings of Jesus. It was a persecuted church. Christians knew that love was the soul of their religion. Then Constantine established Christianity as the State Religion of the Roman Empire, and Orthodoxy became important.

Constantine gave bishops the power to establish what to believe. One of the most powerful bishops was named Augustine, who unfortunately introduced some very harmful doctrines. One was the doctrine of Original Sin, which claimed that because Adam and Eve sinned, we all inherited that sinful nature and are born sinful and unclean. Without baptism, we will go to Hell. He also declared that because Eve sinned first and then tempted Adam, Eve should be submissive to Adam, and all women should be submissive to men. These doctrines came from his interpretation of the story of Adam and Eve.

Augustine's interpretation is flawed. He noticed that the story of Adam and Eve was about sex and temptation, but he missed its primary message. He recognized that the story was symbolic, but he misinterpreted its meaning. We will look at that soon. But first it is helpful to look at the creation stories that are not in the Bible, because the story of Adam and Eve has much in common with them, and is open to the same way of interpretation.

We have already looked at the story of *He Who Holds the Sky with Both Hands*, and have looked at its theme of remembering that we are in the image of the creator. Almost every culture has a story telling how the world began and how humans fit into it. Some of them, like the story of Coyote and Helldiver, seem to be like a fairy tale, used only to entertain. It seems too much like a dream, with animals talking and involved with the creation of the world. It doesn't seem to have the same importance that He Who Holds the Sky has, or that our story of Adam and Eve has. But we will take a look at it and then discuss its importance for us.

Coyote, Fox, and Helldiver the Duck

Once Upon A Time, before there was anything, Coyote was sitting on nothing, doing nothing and thinking about nothing, when along came Fox, prancing along on the nothing. "Hello Coyote," said the fox.

"Hello," said Coyote. And then for a while they said nothing, and did nothing. But then along came Helldiver the Duck, and she too was walking along on nothing. But she stopped short when she saw Coyote and Fox, because she knew that both of them on occasion enjoyed a meal of Fresh Duck.

"Hello Coyote and Fox," she said.

Suddenly Coyote and Fox stopped thinking about nothing, and both of them thought for a minute about Fresh Duck. But then Fox had an idea, and he whispered it to Coyote. Coyote thought about it for a while, and then thought it was a good idea. So he said to Helldiver the Duck, "Helldiver, if you want to live instead of being a meal of Fresh Duck for me and Fox, then I want you to do this. Dive down into the nothing until you find something, and bring it up for us to see."

Afraid of Coyote and Fox, Helldiver dove down into the nothing, as far as she could, and just as she was running out of breath, she bumped into something. She put it into her beak and started swimming up through the nothing until she reached Coyote and Fox, and then she spit it out.

"What is that?" asked Coyote, and Fox, who was about the smartest of all the animals except perhaps Mr. Owl, said "It looks like dirt, or earth, or part of the ground!"

So Coyote said, "Go get some more of it!"

Helldiver the Duck dived down again and brought more of it up, and then more, and then more again, until there was enough earth for everyone to stand on.

Then Coyote said, "Go back down into the nothing as far as you can, and see what else you can bring up."

So Helldiver dove down very deep, and found something else and brought it up. It was water. Coyote and Fox found places to put the water, and the seas and the rivers and the lakes were scattered on the earth, and over the nothing in the spaces between the parts of earth.

Helldiver dove down again, and brought up the bright light that is the sun, and then the little lights of the stars, and then the moon that is not as bright as the sun, but brighter than the stars.

"Go find something else," said the Coyote. So Helldiver dove down and brought up fish to swim in the water, and then other animals to live on the earth.

"More!" said the Coyote, so she dove so deep that she thought she might never get back. And then she found something no one had ever seen before. She brought up a human being. It was so interesting that Fox and Coyote told her to go get another one.

Then the three of them studied this new thing, and Coyote said, "No more! I am afraid this new thing can be dangerous, so we will have only two of them."

Coyote was right, these humans were dangerous. The two that Helldiver brought up were a man and a woman, who became rulers of the land, the water, and everything, including Fox, Coyote, and even Helldiver the Duck. And they seemed to have little regard for life. Not animal life, and they even justified killing each other.

We tend to believe that our Bible is the sacred word of God, and other cultures have only fairy tales. That is part of our human nature, to think that we are right, our religion is true, and they are wrong. We believe that a serpent talked to Adam and Eve, but we think that a talking Coyote and Fox are only a fairy tale. From that point of view, the story of the fox, coyote, and Helldiver seems not to have any real importance other than entertainment.

But looking at it from a different point of view, this story is one explanation of how things became the way they are. One of its implications for us is that we in our culture of mass slaughter of beef, pigs, and chickens have forgotten that all life is sacred, and even animals like foxes and ducks and coyotes raise families. In this story they have an important part in creating the world. To kill them without regard for their lives would not reflect the sacredness of life.

This story helps us realize that we are no longer in relationship with animals — that only in the lives of people like Saint Francis of Assisi or those who choose to be vegetarians in order to spare the lives of animals is there a greater re-membering than what most of us have. In other words, we all experience an alienation from the Garden of Eden, and from the point of view of the animals this alienation can be a matter of life or death.

Chapter Twenty
Pinocchio

I know you are familiar with the story of Pinocchio, but you may not have thought of it as a creation story. It is a fairy tale, but it also is a creation story with a moral, probably more meaningful for us than the story of the Coyote and Fox and Helldiver. It is a symbolic story. We don't really think that Pinocchio was "real." And yet the message makes sense. It is a teaching story showing us in a symbolic way that we are created in the likeness of our Creator, and we are to follow his advice.

In this story, Geppetto, a man, is the creator, a master woodcarver who created many magnificent toys, pieces of furniture, clocks, rocking horses, and other masterpieces made from the very best quality wood. Everything he made was exceptional, but the best and highest of his creations was a wooden puppet, fashioned in the very image and likeness of Geppetto himself, with arms and legs and a human-like face. So far Pinocchio reminds us of the Bible's first story when God created human beings in his own image. But there is a difference. When Pinocchio came to life he was still a piece of wood, -- one that could walk and talk, but nevertheless a puppet without strings. He was not yet a real human being.

The struggle for Pinocchio is to decide which to follow, the advice of Geppetto, his creator, or the inclinations of his wooden puppet nature, a conflict between the flesh (wood) and the spirit. The urges of the body encourage hedonism, giving into what Freud called the Pleasure Principle. But the spirit wants to obey the will of the Creator, of the Father. This is a conflict common to all human beings.

Pinocchio soon finds himself straying from the path set out by Geppetto and instead of going to school, he heads for Stromboli's circus where the need to be center stage and to get applause for the things he can do eventually leads to his being locked in a cage. He has rebelled against his creator, and has to pay the penalty. He has nobody but himself to blame, no woman, no serpent, just himself.

He gets a second chance when a fairy godmother frees him from his cage, but he blows it. First he tells a lie, and discovers that every time he is untruthful his nose grows. His nose becomes a form of biofeedback, something like a polygraph, or lie detector. It reminds me of the biofeedback we get from our dogs when they do something wrong. We can tell immediately by the way their tails drag.

Not only does Pinocchio tell a lie, but he takes the wrong road again, ending up at Pleasure Island, an obvious symbol of a place where people follow the Pleasure Principle. It is here that he begins to change, for the worse. As he smokes cigars, plays pool, and gives into his own sensuality, he becomes more like a jackass and less like a human being, growing a tail and long ears. Worse than that, when he tries to talk, all that comes out is a bray. When this happens he panics, and begins to repent. He realizes that in order to become a real human being instead of a jackass or a puppet, he needs to be in union with his creator. So he begins the arduous search. He goes to the shore of the ocean and brays, "Father!" His father, meanwhile, has been looking for Pinocchio, searching land and sea, and has been swallowed by Monstro the whale.

Geppetto, inside the whale, hears Pinocchio calling for him, and calls back, "Pinocchio!" As he hears this, Pinocchio jumps into the water and risks his life to save Geppetto, to get him out of the belly of the whale. It is this giving of himself that brings about his redemption, and he changes from a donkey not back into a puppet, but into a real boy, a real boy once again in union with his Father.

The message of this story is that we need to be in union with our Creator, or God. But this is a patriarchal story, where God is a man and the "Son of God" is also a male. It does imply that when we are created we are in the image of God, but it also indicates that when we are born we are not fully human. We are made out of wood and are a puppet, not a real human being. So Augustine would likely say that this story supports the idea of Original Sin, that we are born sinful. Pinocchio does stray from the will of his Father, but fortunately he does "repent." One message of the story: Obey your creator or you will turn into a jackass and you will be sorry.

Chapter Twenty One
Six Days of Creation

A lot of people do not realize it, but there are two separate creation stories in the first three chapters of Genesis. The very first Chapter is about God creating the world and everything in it in six days, out of chaos and darkness. God creates the sun, moon, stars, the land and the waters, and every living thing. It is a very old story, reflecting a time even before Abraham.

This story probably wasn't written into the Bible until the time of Solomon, but of course it was told way before that. Who first told it? We don't know. It probably wasn't anyone who was there to see what was happening, at least in the first five days before human beings were created.

In this first story the Hebrew title for God is *Elohim,* a plural form of the word *El,* which is a Hebrew word for "God." Why a plural form? Because there was an ancient time, a time before Abraham, when people thought there were many gods, not just one. The name *Elohim* can mean "gods," or it might mean "God of gods," or "Lord of lords." According to this story, that is who created the world: either the head God of a group of gods, or a group of gods working together. "Let *us* create man in our image," is part of that story as God speaks. In other words, this story allows for more than one God, something that is not allowed after the time of Abraham. This story is therefore before Abraham's time.

Another ancient thing is that in this first story men and women are *both* created in the image of God, as equals. Women are as good as men! Of course that makes sense, but for thousands of years people believed that only men were in the image of God, during a time when patriarchal religion was the dominant religion.

So this first story was about a time before patriarchal religion, a time when people believed in many gods, and when women were equal to men. It was a time when some of the gods were female, and some were male. Woman was made in the image of the female goddesses, and man in the image of the male god. God made them male and female, in the image of *Elohim.*

In the next chapter we will look at the story of Adam and Eve, where male and female are portrayed differently than in the first story. In the Bible's second story of Creation, only Adam is made in God's image.

PART SIX: ADAM AND EVE: A TRADITIONAL INTERPRETATION

Chapter Twenty Two
The Story's Impact on Women's Role

The story of Adam and Eve is our most important creation story as far as its influence on our culture. When people hear the story of Adam and Eve or read it in the Bible they might think something like, "I guess men and women were made for each other. Adam is not complete without his rib; Eve is 'bone of his bone and flesh of his flesh.' It's a story about love between men and women, how much they need each other, and how important God is in their lives. It is the basis for a marriage between one man and one woman, a model set by God."

But *in the Hebrew Scriptures marriage was not only one man and one woman. Powerful men like the kings and patriarchs had many wives. The story of Adam and Eve was not a model for them.*

However, the story did support a patriarchal society and the domination of women by men, a domination that turned into *us against them; men against women.* Men ran the world, women ran the home. That is an unfortunate way to interpret this story, but it is an interpretation that has dominated our thinking for thousands of years.

When man's role was to hunt, defend the family, and produce more children; when women stayed home to have as many children as possible and to raise them, then a patriarchal society would be somewhat understandable. But those factors are not relevant in our society. Things have changed, especially in the last few decades.

When I taught at St. Olaf College in the 1960's, many of the women students said that the main reason they went to college was to find a husband and that their role in life was to be a wife and mother. There of course were exceptions. The nursing students wanted to be nurses, some women wanted to be teachers, and there were others who wanted to have a career. But their focus was mainly different from that of the men, who did not see their role as a husband or father as being their reason for going to college. They wanted college to prepare them for a career as a doctor or scientist or engineer.

Society helped reinforce that idea by encouraging men to focus on a career, as well as paying them higher salaries than women. The television programs like "Leave it to Beaver," and "The Jackie Gleason Show," which were very popular in those days, gave models of the man leaving the home to go to work while the woman stayed home, usually to watch the kids, make the meals, clean the house. But things are different now.

Hillary Clinton, Oprah Winfrey, women astronauts, senators, doctors, clergy, and others have helped us view things differently. But it took a long time. For thousands of years, even up until the past two centuries, most women did not attend school past high school. The message that women should be submissive to men is at least partly responsible for this.

An even worse message of this story is that women are sexual temptations to seduce man away from the will of God.

That is a major motivation for my spending so much time on writing this to you. It is very important to me. I have been a Lutheran minister for almost all of my life, I have invested a lot in the Church. So when I see that it engages in behavior that is not very loving, it is a source of conflict and confusion for me. I want to figure it out so that we can find a way to change.

I have spent a lot of my life (nine years) as a counselor for people who suffered from symptoms of PTSD (Post Traumatic Stress Disorder.) These were people who had suffered from intense trauma. Many were war veterans who had tried to repress the memories of what had happened to them and of what they had done while in combat.

But many of the people who had survived serious trauma were women who had been sexually abused. Many were lesbians. I am not implying that lesbians gave up on men because they were abused and that is why they are lesbians. But what I did learn is that they were some of the most loving people I have ever met. So to abuse them by calling them an abomination is very distressful for me. And it is wrong. I want to be able to voice that, and to stand with you in speaking up for them and for all people who are victims of prejudice. And I believe the story of Adam and Eve is a support, the way it has been interpreted, for treating women as inferior to men. That story has been very misinterpreted and misused, putting down women as victims of prejudice. I want to stand with you, with Gail, and with Laurie, Mary, and Julie to help right this wrong.

God becomes Male

In the story of Adam and Eve, men are created in God's image, but women are not. God and Adam are both male; Eve is not. And the Male God, whose name is now known as *Yahweh Elohim* is One God. Eve is to obey both the male God and Adam; a woman is therefore to obey the male God, her father, and her husband. Eve is the weaker part of human nature, easily tempted by Satan (the serpent in this story has been interpreted to be a symbol for Satan) whereas Adam, the man, would have been obedient to the Lord's commands if he had not been tempted by Eve. Therefore all women are to be submissive to their husbands, as they will lead them to obey God. At least that is the way many people have understood this story, led to this interpretation by the "Fathers of the Church."

Martin Luther is only one of many men who have used the story of Adam and Eve to put down women. I think basically he was a good man, but he sure made a mistake here. The following quote is from *Lectures on Genesis*. If you are interested, you can find it in Volume 1 of *Luther's Works*, edited by Jaroslav Pelikan. (See bibliography).

Satan's cleverness is perceived also in this, that he attacks the weak part of the human nature, Eve the woman, not Adam the man. ... I believe that if he had tempted Adam first, the victory would have been Adam's. He would have crushed the serpent with his foot and would have said, "Shut up! The Lord's command was different."

Wow!

It is clear: According to the interpretation of important men, God wills that Men Rule. The men who created this interpretation were powerful, important religious leaders like St. Augustine, a bishop and theologian of the early Christian Church. In his book *The Literal Meaning of Genesis,* he writes that woman was made *for the man from the man. … Whoever calls these facts into question* **undermines all that we believe**, *and his opinions should be resolutely cast out of the minds of the faithful.*

In other words, it is an essential matter of faith, according to Augustine, that we believe woman was made for the man; Eve was made to be a helpmate for Adam and man is to rule over her. This was a central teaching of the Hebrew Scriptures, of the Quran, and of the Christian Patriarchs. It is a teaching that lasted until the 20th Century.

Seduction

Another teaching is that women are evil, likely to tempt men away from God. God tells them that they must not eat of the fruit of the tree of knowledge, or they will die. But Eve, knowing God's commandment, nevertheless decides to eat of the fruit when an erect serpent tells her that she will not die if she eats of it, but instead she will become like God, knowing good and evil. Not only does she eat, but she gives Adam the fruit and he also eats. Death now will touch them because of what she did.

When Adam and Eve ate the fruit of the Tree of Knowledge, both realized that they were naked, and they lost their innocence and became ashamed. They hid from the Lord God, but He found them and punished them for their disobedience. Eve blamed the serpent for their behavior, Adam blamed Eve. But God holds them responsible for their own behavior and tells them the consequences. Adam will now have to toil for his food by the sweat of his brow, and Eve will bear children in pain. And because Eve made a bad decision and then tempted Adam, she will be subject to him. He will make the decisions. He will rule. He is now the master of the house, the captain of the ship.

Adam and Eve are then banished from the Garden of Eden, never to return. In case they try, angels guard the entrance. The punishment for the serpent is that he will no longer walk erect, but will crawl on his belly, and there will be enmity between him and the woman.

That is the story and its traditional interpretation, an interpretation that has caused a lot of harm, especially to women.

Chapter Twenty Three
Men Are Meant To Control Women?

The Hebrew Scriptures have many passages that support the superiority of men, all taken from the patriarchal point of view, most supported by the story of Adam and Eve. All of them divide the world into two groups: the superior man and the inferior woman.

For instance, Exodus 20:17 states that a woman is the property of her husband:

You shall not covet (be jealous of, want to possess, desire) your neighbor's house; you shall not covet your neighbor's wife, or his manservant, or his maidservant, or his ox, or his donkey, or anything that is your neighbor's.

It is clear that this commandment is given to the man, that he should not desire his neighbor's wife because she belongs to her husband. There is no indication that a wife is on a different level than the donkey or the ox of his neighbor. He shall covet none of them. The wife belongs to the husband, the woman to the man.

That a man is superior to a woman and should rule over her are thoughts not only from the Hebrew Scriptures, but also from the Christian Scriptures:

Let a woman learn in silence with all submissiveness. I permit no woman to teach or to have authority over men; she is to keep silent. For Adam was formed first, then Eve, and Adam was not deceived, but the woman was deceived and became a transgressor (1 Tim. 2:11-14).

In the patriarchal society, even including the Christian Church, this statement by Paul (or by one of his disciples) has been used to forbid the ordination of women to the priesthood or to the ministry, for they should not teach or have authority over men. They are to keep silent. But Paul adds the way a woman in a patriarchal society might be saved:

Yet women will be saved through bearing children, if she continues in faith and love and holiness, with modesty (1 Tim. 2:15).

Nicole, by now you are probably getting angry, and you have a right to be. But unfortunately, it gets worse:

Tertullian, an early leader of the Christian Church, wrote of women:

You are the devil's gateway, you are the unsealer of that forbidden tree, you are the first deserter of the divine law, you are the one who persuaded him whom the devil was too weak to attack. How easily you destroyed man, the image of God! Because of the death which you brought upon us, even the Son of God had to die. (This quote and other interesting things can be found in a book by Paul Jewett, called *Man as Male and Female*. It's listed at the back.)

Just imagine! A leader of the Christian Church writing that a woman is the devil's gateway who destroyed man, the image of God! What nonsense! And it is because of woman that even the Son of God had to die! That's as bad as blaming the Jews for killing Jesus. And not only blaming the Jews of 2000 years ago, but blaming their ancestors. That is what happened to women. For thousands of years they were considered to be a temptation because a story written thousands of years ago said that Eve was!

All of this and much more are derived from the story of Adam and Eve as it has been interpreted by Augustine and other *fathers* of faith. Nancy Van Vuuren provides many quotations from the church fathers regarding the role of women in her book *The subversion of women as practiced by Churches, witch-hunters and other sexists.*

I haven't included any more of those quotes because I think by now you have had enough. The examples I have already given should suffice to show that the story of Adam and Eve has been used for the evil purpose of making women submit to the control of men, much as the Taliban right now in Afghanistan are using the Quran to justify their domination of women. Maybe things will change there, if the Taliban are defeated again. We will have to see how that war will go in Afghanistan.

For some traditional patriarchal societies such as Afghanistan under the rule of the Taliban the women are not allowed to read and write, to teach, or to have authority over men. They need to comply with the man's wishes, whether the father or the husband, or sometimes even the brother. Even now there are societies that permit the killing of women who "dishonor" the family by having sexual relationships outside of marriage, even if they are raped. This practice is known in English as "Honor Killing."

Witchcraft Trials

The degradation of women reached its height (or perhaps depth is a better word, for it reaches a very low point) during the witchcraft trials that lasted for approximately 400 years, from the mid 1300's to the mid 1700's. These trials were influenced by the words of Augustine who said that when Eve was seduced by the serpent, the serpent was acting as a vehicle for the devil, and that the serpent is also a phallic symbol (a symbol of the penis.) This led to the view that women are so lustful that they cannot resist the serpent-phallus-devil, interchangeable symbols. Witchcraft was then thought to be the effect of a woman having intercourse with the devil. "Witches" were killed for this crime, based on "evidence" that no one would think of as real. Imagine that! The story of Adam and Eve used to actually kill women!

Women and the Word of God, Even Today

A friend of mine is an ordained Lutheran minister who was one of the first women ordained in the ELCA. She told me that the President of the Synod asked her to join him for lunch before the ordination took place, and at the luncheon he told her that if she had the best interests of the Church in her heart, she would decline ordination. If the ELCA ordained women, it would interfere with the relationships we had with other churches that were against women having any authority over men. It was pretty intimidating, because he was at that time the leader of the Lutheran Church.

It had to do with the Bible, he said. She could be responsible for the division that would be sure to come between us and the Lutherans who thought we were acting against the word of God. She discovered later that the other female seminary graduates received a similar lunch invitation, and they gave the same response as hers: they walked out on him and were ordained. They have all become superb examples of Christian ministers.

But the conflict between churches still goes on. In 2004 I attended a conference in Chicago for Lutheran ministers involved in Lutheran social ministries. Representatives from the two largest Lutheran bodies in the United States were involved. But we could not share a worship service with communion because we who were members of the ELCA (Evangelical Lutheran Church of America) had ordained women for ministry.

So we who were Lutherans of the wrong persuasion were excommunicated (not allowed to commune with, to receive communion with) from those who thought of us as *them*. It made us feel as though we were inferior – a feeling gay people and many women in the church had shared for a long time, at least until women were allowed to be ordained, an event that happened in 1970. This split among churches is happening again now because some churches accept gay and lesbian people, as well as women, for ordination.

How we understand the Bible is important. In the following chapter I'll suggest an interpretation for the story of Adam and Eve that would have made a lot of difference if it had been understood that way during the last two thousand years. This interpretation regards woman as man's equal, and considers sexuality a blessing rather than a curse.

PART SEVEN: ADAM AND EVE NOW

Chapter Twenty Four
A Symbolic Interpretation

The story of Adam and Eve is a symbolic story, and it can be interpreted in the same way we might interpret the creation stories we have already looked at. They are stories about us.

Even though what I am about to say goes against the traditional understanding of this story, I believe that the story of Adam and Eve is *not* a condemnation of women; it is not a story telling us that we are born sinful and unclean; and it is not a story telling us that sex is the original sin

The story of Adam and Eve *is* a story about *our* creation, about our conception and birth, when we were created "in the Garden of Eden," and when we were expelled from that garden at our birth. For approximately the first nine months of life we lived in this garden, a comfortable place where our life was nourished and where we were safe. All of our food was freely given through the umbilical cord, and we do not have to toil for it. We are connected to mother's body, a source of warmth. We hear the comforting rhythmic beat of her heart and we hear her voice. The womb is our own Garden of Eden, a place where we are nurtured as we grow. This could be a new idea for you, but think about it.

Our life began when a naked man and a naked woman, like Adam and Eve, who symbolize all men and all women, were tempted to eat from the fruit of the tree in the midst of the garden, which was named the Tree of *Knowledge*. In Hebrew, the word "to know" (*yadah*) has as a primary meaning the way a man knows a woman through sexual intercourse. In other words, eating of the fruit of this tree is a symbol for when Adam knew Eve in a very intimate way, the act very closely associated with our being in the womb: The cause of our being there.

For our mother, (Eve in this story is a symbol of the mother of all life) the tempter was something erect that looked a lot like a serpent. For our father (Adam as a symbol of the first man, the ancestor of us all), it was a fruit offered by the woman (the Bible does not mention an apple, but that is what people often think of.) Then, after the seduction (temptation) of the woman by the erect serpent and of the man by the woman, the man and the woman knew they were naked and got dressed, covering their nakedness. The serpent now is no longer erect but crawls along the earth. The man would now toil for his food and the woman would be cursed by God, a curse that can be translated in various ways. In the Revised Standard Version of the Bible the curse is this:

*To the woman he said, "I will greatly multiply your pain in childbearing; in pain you shall bring forth children, yet your desire shall be for your husband, and **he shall rule over you.**"* (Genesis 3:16)

This translation supports the traditional interpretation offered by Augustine, that the man rules and the woman is to be submissive. But here is another equally valid translation, in *The Book of J* by David Rosenberg, a well-known and respected Hebrew scholar. I like his interpretation, of course, because it fits perfectly with my idea of what the story of Adam and Eve is about:

To the woman he said: "Pain increasing, groans that spread into groans: having children will be labor. To your man's body your belly will rise, for he will be eager above you."

This translation of Genesis 3:16 relates God's "curse" to the theme of sexuality and of childbirth.

Pain increasing, groans that spread into groans, having children will be labor.

That is clearly what happens to most women during labor and delivery. They deliver their baby with "labor pains." Don't let that scare you too much, because if you get married and have children you will find that modern medicine has ways to help you avoid a lot of the pain usually associated with childbirth.

To your man's body your belly will rise, for he will be eager above you.

This translation by David Rosenberg is related to the sexuality that causes conception, labor, and delivery – not to the idea that a woman should be submissive to a man because he is superior and she is inferior, but to her passion for her husband and his for her: *To your man's body your belly will rise, for he will be eager above you.*

There are two good things about this translation. The first is that it does not put women into submission to men. The second is that it does not make sex linked up to the devil, as a source of sin. Of course sex can be and often is misused, just as nuclear power is often used for bombs instead of providing electricity for cities. We misuse a lot of the blessings we have. But the point is that sex is meant to be a blessing that accompanies love and the creation of children. That is a reason why the Bible might mention it, even at the beginning.

Even the curse in the Bible that man has to toil for his food is related to the expulsion from Eden. When the woman gives birth, the baby (little Adam) for the first time in his life has to toil for his food which up until that time has been freely given through the umbilical cord in the garden of pleasure and nurture. Expulsion from Eden is our expulsion from the womb and the beginning of our toil for food. Now the child has to nurse at her breast, which is hard work for a newborn.

The point is this: No longer can this story be a story of Eve tempting Adam. No longer can it be a message that sex is related to the devil. It is a story of what happens when a man and woman love and desire each other so that they help a new life begin.

Chapter Twenty Five
The Serpent is a Symbol of Eternal Life, and of Sexual Temptation

The serpent was a symbol of eternal life because it shed its skin and kept on living, seemingly forever; shedding one skin after another while it continued to live. (The idea is something like the idea of reincarnation, that a person keeps living forever, just taking on new bodies.) The serpent is also a symbol of the male sexual organ.

For the Hebrews, the male organ was a reservoir of life, containing the seeds of life. (The word "sperm" comes from the Greek word meaning "seed.") They thought that the man sowed the seed into the woman who was like a fertile earth that allowed the seed to grow. This, of course, made the man seem like the source of life, and the woman the one who nurtured it.

For the Hebrews, circumcision symbolized the shedding of the skin in the same way the serpent did, providing a symbol of life that continues even past the leaving behind of the external body.

Circumcision for the Hebrews was also a sign of the covenant with God and a way for the child to be incorporated into the tribe as one of God's chosen people, a descendant of Abraham, Isaac, and Jacob. The problem is that only males could be circumcised. It left women out of the covenant. That is why now, for Christians, baptism replaces circumcision. Baptism invites women as well as men to join the covenant to be a part of the Body of Christ. This is a step away from patriarchal religion, giving women equal status with men.

Here is the point I am trying to make: If the erect serpent is a symbol of a sexually aroused male, then it is no longer Eve who is to blame for being seduced, and the devil has nothing to do with the story. If there is a seduction, it is Adam who tempts Eve, nor the devil.

After the seduction by the symbol of the erect male, the "serpent" crawls in the dust. At this point the seduction is over. Adam and Eve put on their fig leafs, both of them knowing that this seductive or passionate behavior won't happen until the serpent becomes erect again.

Adam Comes From *Adam*ah: Man Comes From Mother Earth

The traditional interpretation of this story is that Adam gave birth to Eve, and therefore men are superior to women as the giver of life, and should rule over them. But in this story (in the original Hebrew) there is an indication that the feminine Mother Earth is in fact the source of life.

Adam is a Hebrew masculine noun that means man, or mankind. But Adam is made from *Adamah*, a feminine noun that means "earth, or soil." *Adamah* is the feminine form of *Adam*. Adam comes from Adamah, the male from the female Mother Earth.

This, of course, fits what we observe. Woman gives birth to all human life.

Chapter Twenty Six
Eve is Not a Servant for Adam, But Represents God

The word *ezer* is often translated as "helpmate," and has been interpreted to mean that Eve is not man's equal, but his servant. Adam was alone, so God made for him a helpmate (*ezer*). *The same Hebrew word that is translated as "helpmate" and which refers to Eve is the word that throughout the Old Testament refers also to God.* In fact, most of the time it is used to refer to God. In Psalm 46, for instance: "God is our refuge and strength, a very present *help* in trouble." Again, in Deuteronomy 33:26: "There is none like God, ... who rides through the heavens to your *help*."

The word *ezer* does not imply being in an inferior or submissive position. On the contrary, it implies being in a position of strength and superiority, as is true of God. This word does not refer to the helpmate whose place is in the kitchen, whose role is to bring slippers and a drink to the Lord of the manor who sits in a rocking chair by the fireplace. It is meant to indicate that Eve, and therefore all women, are a source of love, of strength, of goodness, beauty, or any other attribute that God has as our *ezer*. Terence Fretheim states in the book *Creation, fall, and Flood*:

> *The word "helper" or "helpmeet" is used primarily in the Old Testament for God himself (See Dt. 33:7, 26). Man is in need of someone to be a representative of God at his side.*

This puts an entirely different interpretation on the role of woman. If she is to be a representative of God at the side of man, this is certainly a different role than to be his inferior, his servant. In fact, if she is God's representative at Adam's side then she is in partnership with God and if anything, Adam's superior rather than inferior.

Nicole, this makes so much sense to me. Often it is a woman who helps nourish a man's spirituality, whether as mother or as wife.

Chapter Twenty Seven
Birth, Original Sin, and Butt Dust

If the Garden of Eden is a symbol for the womb, then expulsion from the Garden of Eden is a symbol of birth. In other words, we were not expelled from the Garden of Eden because Adam and Eve sinned. We were expelled because it was a time to be born.

That puts a whole new interpretation of "Original Sin." I'm not sure if you have ever heard those words, original sin, but that idea has influenced people for well over a thousand years. It is the idea that we are born sinful; that we inherit the sin of Adam and Eve who disobeyed God by eating the fruit of the tree of knowledge. In some churches during Lent, (the time before Easter) on Ash Wednesday people will come to the altar rail and have ashes put on their forehead as a symbol of being sinful. Here is one story about that:

We Are Butt Dust

When Jacob was five years old he was taken to an Ash Wednesday service which began the season of Lent. During part of the service he and his parents, along with everyone else, came to the altar rail where he kneeled and the pastor marked his forehead with ashes and said, "Remember that you are but dust, and to dust you shall return." When the church service was over and they were on their way home, Jacob asked his mother, "Mommy, what is butt dust?"

Butt dust. That is a good picture of what is meant by original sin in its original interpretation by Augustine. And of Sigmund Freud's interpretation.

We Are But Dust

When he was a small child, Sigmund Freud was walking with his father on a sidewalk in Vienna when a stranger approached and knocked the hat off his father's head. To Sigmund's surprise, his father picked his hat out of the gutter and walked on as if nothing had happened. When he asked his father about it, his dad said, "You see, that man is a gentile. We're Jews. It's better to just take it than to get into trouble."

When Sigmund told his mother what had happened and she saw how disappointed he was in his father's behavior she said, "Here's something you need to know, Sigmund. People are basically evil. It's because they are made out of dirt. Let me show you." And she began rubbing her hands together, palm against palm, until two little bits of dirt emerged between her palms. She showed that to Sigmund. "That is how God made us," she said, referring to the story of Adam and Eve where God creates Adam from the dust of the earth. We are but dust, and to dust we shall return.

That experience profoundly affected Freud and his theory of human nature. The humiliation of his father at the hands of the Gentile followed by mother's demonstration of the story from the Bible that we are made of dirt -- this combination of factors established firmly in his mind that people are basically selfish, controlled by their passions and instinct for *self* preservation.

As early as the fourth century the Church labeled sex as the Original Sin, a curse rather than a blessing, something to be tightly controlled. And yet sex provides a very intimate form of love, allowing a man and woman to know each other so intensely that the Bible says they become "one flesh." Sex provides a way for the race to survive through the transmission of our DNA to the next generation by creating a new child. Sex is a wonderful blessing. But it is such a strong instinct to be sexual, that it is a very difficult force to control.

Many priests are healthy adults offering a ministry of love and grace to their congregations. My mentor and hero, Bishop Shannon, is one of these. However, because priests have been told by the Roman Catholic Church that they must be celibate, that sex would otherwise taint their lives with sin, they have thus been denied a vital form of intimacy. Consequently some of them (even one would be too many) have replaced love with lust, and intimacy with abusive relationships, including child abuse. As a result the Catholic Church has paid out over one billion dollars to victims of abuse by clergy, enough to cause some dioceses to file for bankruptcy.

Chapter Twenty Eight
Immersion In Love?

When I was a pastor in Bellevue, Washington I received a call from a man whose grandson, age four months, had just died. He was healthy when his mother put him to bed, but when she woke in the morning he was dead, from Sudden Infant Death Syndrome (SIDS).

She called her parents to let them know what had happened, and then, because she was so choked up with grief, she asked her husband to call their minister, to tell him of the tragedy and to ask if he would come to help them in their grief. But the pastor refused.

He sadly told them that they hadn't baptized their boy yet, and so he could not offer any hope or consolation for them. Nor could he in good conscience participate in the funeral because he did not believe an unbaptized baby would go to Heaven! He believed in the doctrine of original sin which states that we are all born sinful and unclean, in need of baptism in order to find salvation. It would be better to find another pastor, he said

A few hours later her father called me. His voice was so choked with sobs that it was hard to understand him. He asked if I could officiate at the little boy's funeral and if I could meet with the family who lived just a few miles from my office.

This tragic example of *us vs. them*, the baptized vs. the unbaptized, caused almost as much pain to the already distraught and grieving mother as if her baby had been killed as a heretic. Baptism is meant to be an immersion into an ocean or river of love flowing from God the Father, God the Son, and God the Holy Spirit. This immersion in the love of God actually begins even before the birth of the baby, but baptism is a celebration that this love continues after birth. Sadly, this is something their minister did not understand.

Chapter Twenty Nine
Birth Trauma and Baptism

The Garden of Eden is a perfect 98.6 degrees, body temperature. Adam is surrounded by fluids, now called amniotic fluids, but referred to in the Bible as rivers. These protect Adam from bumps and injury, acting as a cushion between him and the outside world. The womb is a pleasurable garden of delight. Adam is aware that he is not alone. There is the sound of mother's heartbeat and there is a life-sustaining force surrounding the baby. Mother's body becomes for Adam a revelation of God, a source of comfort, love, life, safety, and warmth. Her body in fact is the source of his life and nurture. But then comes what sometimes has been referred to as "the Fall," meaning the fall from grace as we are expelled from Eden.

The contractions begin, and little Adam is forced through the cervix into the narrow birth canal which squeezes his head into the shape of a raindrop. Luckily, he has six soft spots on his head, called fontanelles, which allow the head to emerge without damage.

But then there are bad things that happen. He is now separated from the source of his life and his food and his warmth, and put out into the cold. The umbilical cord is cut, and he is alienated, never again able to return to that particular Paradise, though as a grown man he will try to enter while making love. "He drove out the man, and at the east of Eden he placed the Cherubim, and a flaming sword which turned every way, to guard the tree of life" (Gen 3:24). Now when he is hungry he has to toil for his food, sucking either at mother's breast or at the nipple of a bottle. It is hard work, and a newborn Adam or Eve is soon exhausted while feeding. He or she needs clothes now to guard against the cold and to cover his nakedness. No longer are there amniotic fluids to cushion him from the bumps and bruises of life, for he is alone. No longer does he hear the reassuring rhythm of the mother's heartbeat, for he is separated from her, estranged and alienated.

In other words, the baby is born into a state of what Augustine called original sin, which is just another way of saying the baby is born into a state of separation, or alienation from mother and the womb. This alienation is also referred to as our "Fall" or expulsion from Eden.

For almost two thousand years the Christian Church has had a symbolic way to deal with this alienation. The remedy is to be immersed in love. The Church has a rite when a person is incorporated into the body of "Holy Mother the Church," or into the "Body of Christ" through baptism. That is the symbolic meaning of baptism.

Later in life, sex becomes a symbolic way of meeting the needs of the alienated person. Sex is a way for a man to again feel "one flesh" with a woman, symbolically bringing him back to the original state of grace in the Garden of Eden. It is a way for him to re-enter the womb and connect with the warmth and nurture there. It is a way for a man not to feel so lonely. But for the newborn baby, the immersion in love is symbolized by being immersed in water, or in many churches, by having water sprinkled on the baby's forehead.

Unfortunately, the symbol has been used to condemn people who have not had this rite performed. They are then not one of us. But like many symbols, this one has been misinterpreted and misused. If it were understood as immersion in love, its abuse would be less likely.

PART EIGHT: SO WHAT CAN WE DO?

Chapter Thirty
We Can Choose

So Nicole, it may seem that the odds are against us. Our instinct for self-preservation has made us suspicious of strangers, those who do not seem to be one of *us*. That has made us divide the world into *us against them*. Often war has been the result. Since the time of Constantine, even the Church has seemed to be an organization of *us against* them, *Christians against non-Christians*; or sometimes even *one denomination of Christianity against another*.

But we have also seen that the teachings of Jesus are about love, and that for the first 300 years of Christianity, people seemed to be able to choose love, regardless of the consequences. We can do the same, you and I and everyone else. We can find a way to control our own behavior, regardless what other people do. We can choose love. This is the basic message of Christianity, that we love one another, regardless of what other people do. As the nations of the world become nuclear powers and as China emerges as a united modern nation this becomes even more important now than it has ever been.

Four Events That Impact Our Lives

There is a theory of psychology which explains why it is so important for us to control our own behavior, regardless of what other people do. This theory has been developed by Dr. Frank Gerbode, whose book *Beyond Psychology: An Introduction to Metapsychology* is the best resource I know to explain what I mean, but the following summary states the general idea.

According to this theory, **there are four important events that can impact a person's well-being:**

1. **Things that other people do to other people**, observed or made known to us. This includes both good and bad things. We may know of an attack on the Twin Towers

and the deaths of many people. This may impact us greatly, bringing fear or sorrow to us. Or we may know of organizations or people who have shown love or who, like the Bill and Melinda Gates Foundation, have brought vaccines, healthcare, and education to those who need it. This can give us hope and encouragement. Though things that other people do to other people do greatly affect us, the impact is likely not to be as great as

2. **Things that other people do to *us*.** They might show us love, in which case we can be encouraged or inspired, invited to live. Or they might attack us, in which case we will be angered or frightened, possibly even killed. What happens to us can be of vital importance.

One category that is sometimes overlooked is how role models impact us. When Tiger Woods or President Clinton engage in sexual affairs with a mistress, that affects us. It makes it seem more acceptable. Or when Shaun White (or for my generation Mark Spitz) excels in the Olympic Games, it makes us think that excellence might be possible for us.

Bishop Shannon is a role model for me, as is Desmond Tutu. They provide examples of excellence that I strive for because I see the value of their integrity. Jesus, of course, is such an example that has affected the lives of countless people.

3. **Things that we do to other people.** We might help other people or hurt them, befriend them or attack them. If we help and befriend them we are likely to enhance our feelings of self-worth as well as expect nurturing behaviors from those we have befriended. We will view them as potential friends and allies. On the other hand, if we hurt or attack them we are likely to expect some kind of retaliation. We may be more fearful and more likely to view them as enemies who will hurt us. Sometimes even if we kill other people and get away with it, knowing we will never receive retaliation, nevertheless we can pay a high price from our own conscience. We may be afraid that we will be

discovered, or have nightmares, or feel guilt. Sometimes this is the primary cause for Post Traumatic Stress Disorder.

4. **Things we do to ourselves**. We may hurt or help ourselves. If our self-image is negative we are likely to criticize ourselves and put ourselves in situations that bring about hurtful consequences. We may not feel we are worthy of leadership or even of friendship. Our expectation will be that others will feel the same about us as we feel about ourselves. Alienation from others can cause even suicide. But if we take good care of ourselves, act with integrity, nurture our feelings of self-worth, and respond to others from a place of worth, then we are likely to be at peace with ourselves.

Surprisingly, how we treat ourselves is the most important of the four, unless what other people do to us includes killing us. And even dying with integrity might be better than living without a soul.

PTSD and War

I'm not sure if you know this, because you were pretty young during those years, but for nine years of my life my primary responsibility was to bring healing to lives damaged by trauma; to counsel with survivors of Post Traumatic Stress Disorder. Some of these people were survivors of an automobile accident in which others were killed, or people who had survived a hurricane, or parents whose babies had died of SIDS (Sudden Infant Death Syndrome). But the majority of the people I worked with during those years were either veterans of the Vietnam War or women who had been raped or sexually abused as children.

In war all four of the influences mentioned above are likely to be more negative than positive. A soldier may have a sense that he is helping defend our own country, our families and countrymen. That is a force for good, and is something he is doing for others. He will also be bonded to the people who are in his military unit, a powerful way to become one of *us*.

But what a soldier sees other people doing to other people will include ways in which they try to and sometimes succeed in killing each other. What other people are doing to us in combat is attacking us. What we are doing to other people often involves us shooting at them or killing them if we are in combat. None of these are good for our life or our self-image. They are all negative influences, influences that have caused many people to despair, even to kill themselves. I have heard the estimate that as many people killed themselves by 1990 as a result of what happened to them and what they did during the Vietnam War that ended in 1975 as those who were killed during the war and whose names are on the Vietnam War Memorial Wall.

For many people who developed symptoms of PTSD, the symptoms are maintained mainly by a sense of guilt.

In order to explain what I mean, it is important to define guilt. Guilt is not only a feeling that we have done something wrong, though sometimes this is true. Guilt, the emotion that maintains symptoms of PTSD, is the result of unfulfilled intentions. Another way of saying this is that guilt is the result of failure to fulfill a purpose. The more basic the purpose, the stronger the guilt. Guilt is not always the result of doing something evil or wrong. Often it is the result of failing to do what we are meant to do, or what we intend to do.

Our basic intention is to live according to our basic nature as people created in the image of God.

Chapter Thirty One
Our Purpose in Life

We all have a purpose in life, and we are happiest when we discover that purpose and take steps toward fulfilling it. That is the point of the following story. I think it is a story told by Carl Jung, but I haven't been able to verify that by searching through his writings, so it may have come from a lecture I heard when I was a student many years ago. The story goes like this:

Kindling the Sacred Fire on the Mountain

Once there was a very wise and curious man who was very interested in what it was that made for a happy and healthy community. He searched throughout Europe and the United States and Africa, looking for a tribe or group of people who lived with joy, with love, and with peace. When he found a group that had these characteristics, he would investigate whether they also seemed aware of and interested in the welfare of people who were not members of that community.

His search took him many years, and he found many communities that had some of the things he was looking for. But the one community that seemed to be a model of human life at its best was a group of Native Americans in the southwestern part of the United States.

The tribe not only cared for each other, they were also a religious people who believed that God had put them on earth to call the sun from the darkness of night to bring light to the day for all people everywhere. In order to do this, they had a team of three people who climbed the mountain that towered above their valley. Every night shortly after midnight this team of three would climb the mountain. One person would carry the kindling, another would carry the larger pieces of wood to turn the kindling into a bright flame, and the third person would carry the flint and the tinder needed to light the fire. They believed that when they lit the fire at the top of the mountain (not a tall mountain like Mount Rainier or Mount Baker, but one that would be more like our foothills in Washington State) the fire would coax the sun from its place of rest.

Every week the team would be replaced by three different people in the tribe, because they wanted every person to be able to participate in this necessary work, one that would bring the sun to all people everywhere, giving its light, warmth, and power for the plants to grow.

This was a religious calling for them, uniting them to God, to each other, and to the whole world. They felt called by God, and knew they were a blessing to all of humankind. As a result, they had a sense of value, and they also respected each other as people called by God to bless the whole world. They lived in love, peace, and joy.

The wise man believed that they were the most healthy people on the planet, and he wrote a book about his results.

Because many people read his book, the tribe became famous and many people came to visit them, to take their picture, and to interact with them. Some of these tourists did what you might think. They laughed at the belief that these people had the power to bring the sun to light and warm the earth.

So eventually the people of this tribe began to doubt their calling, and as you might guess, there came a time when one of the people put it to the test. He carried the tinder with his team. The tinder was needed to ignite the fire. But halfway up the mountain, in the dark, he threw the tinder off the side of the mountain, much to the horror of the other two.

As they waited, wondering what would happen, the sun came up even though they were unable to light the fire.

As a result, many of the people lost their faith and became discouraged. They began to accept the ways of the world, and became enamored of *things* and money and values that didn't have much at all to do with helping the world or bringing light into the darkness, or love or peace or joy.

But the man who had thrown the tinder down the side of the mountain lit a candle in his own home every morning, keeping alive in his own heart the idea of the Sacred Fire.

This is a wisdom story, and for us it is about our purpose in life.

Our purpose in life is to live with integrity as people created in the Image of God. We are meant to live in love, to seek what is holy, to let our light shine, and to invite others to live. That is built into us. When we are not able to do this, we will suffer alienation from our very self, from our soul. *This is Very Important to know.*

When we have a goal, another way to talk about it is to say that we have an intention. Our basic intention is also what we call our purpose in life.

Usually our basic intention or purpose in life is lived in relationship to others. Parents, for example, have the basic intention to invite their children to live, to keep them safe, to nurture them. If they fail, they will feel extreme anxiety, sorrow, or dis-ease. Another word for this dis-ease is guilt. That does not mean we have done something wrong, it just means that we are not on track to fulfill our basic intention.

If a child dies, the parent will feel not only sorrow and anger, but will feel guilty. It is not that the parent is to blame for the death. A parent is totally blameless in the accidental or unexplained death of a child in a SIDS death, for instance. But even though the parents are totally blameless, they have a very strong intention to protect their child, to keep it safe from harm, to support the child's survival. If the child dies, this intention is frustrated, and the parents feel guilty. Failure equates with guilt for them. The failure to keep the child safe feels like guilt, as if they were somehow responsible for the death, even when they are not.

The same is true for the person in charge when troops under their command are killed in war, or if they were the driver of a car or boat or plane which crashed and a passenger was killed, even when it has been demonstrated that they were not personally at fault. The engineer of a train can be almost destroyed with guilt if he hits a person on the tracks who is clearly committing suicide by train. A police officer can carry guilt for shooting a robber in self defense. These symptoms are another indication that people want to view themselves as good, as guardians of life. Their intention is to protect life, not to take it. When that intention is not fulfilled, guilt is the result, regardless of the innocence of that person. And guilt is a primary cause of Post Traumatic Stress Disorder (PTSD).

Peter's Unfulfilled Intention

We will call him Peter. He was commissioned as a 2nd Lieutenant in the Army during a time when the fighting was most severe during the Vietnam war. He disobeyed his orders to take his platoon on search and destroy missions, and instead he and the men under his command sat in a circle with their backs to trees. They put a wire around the perimeter, so that when the wire would be tripped by the enemy in the jungle, claymore mines would explode outward, protecting them. That was his basic intention. He wanted to protect his troops, to bring everyone in his platoon back home safely.

But one night Peter heard an explosion. The next thing he was aware of was a voice saying, "Wait a minute. I thing this one is alive!" It was dark, but then there was a sound as if something was tearing. It was the body bag being unzipped. All the men in his platoon had been killed when the Viet Cong overran their position. Only he remained alive, but already in a body bag.. He had failed to protect his men so they could return to the States alive. So, despite the fact that he did everything in his power to protect his men, he carried the guilt of failure and developed symptoms of PTSD.

It is not that Peter did something wrong that made him feel guilty. It was just that he was unable to fulfill his intention to keep hs men safe.

The Hungry Hyena

Sometimes we have two intentions that want to take us in two completely different directions, causing a problem because we don't know which way to go. That is what happens in the following story:

Once a hyena on the Serengeti Plain was very hungry. Fortunately, he smelled the fragrance of a dead animal, and he turned toward the smell. But as he did so, he caught the fragrance of another dead animal in exactly the opposite direction. First he turned toward one, but when he did so it seemed that he was going farther away from the other, and regardless which way he turned it seemed he would miss out on onc of the meals. The pull in each direction was so strong that he was pulled apart, half in one direction and half in the other. Split in two, he died.

Going Off Track

The same basic story as the hyena was told to me by a man who came to me for counseling.

He told me of a dream that kept recurring. He was in his attic where he had an elaborate train set, with steam engines and diesel engines pulling passenger cars, freight cars, oil tankers, and other kinds of rolling stock. But in his dream the different engines ran into each other, knocking them all off the track. He said there was something disturbing about the dream.

I asked him what it made him think of. He thought for a minute and then became nervous or embarrassed. Finally he said that it made him think of an affair he was having. He loved his wife, and wanted to have his family. But he also loved his mistress. He said, "I think my life is going off track."

To get back on track, he decided to tell his mistress that he was choosing his family, and they were going to have to end the affair.

When he did this, he no longer felt "off track," or what I could also think of as "being pulled in two directions at once," or even "being pulled in two."

Like the hyena, the Lakota warrior, or the man going off track, we know the experience of being in conflict between right and wrong, and we need to choose what to do. In the next chapters I am including stories of people who chose what is right, with the hope that their stories will inspire you in the same way they inspired me.

Chapter Thirty Two
Desmond Tutu:
The Unlikely Power of Love
and Forgiveness

To carry anger and resentment rather than forgiveness is like taking poison thinking that it will kill the one you resent.
Depak Chopra, quoting Gandhi

I have already mentioned that Desmond Tutu and Bishop Shannon are role models for me. In this chapter and the next, I want to explain why.

If everyone in the world loved each other and refused to let hatred or murder into their lives, the world would be a far better, more peaceful place. That is such an obvious truth that no reasonable person would deny its truth. But our instinct for self-preservation urges us to hate and kill our enemies instead of loving them. We seem to feel safer that way. If we belong to the White Hat Theology we feel threatened by the Black Hat People because they are different. But this can be a self-fulfilling prophecy, because if we hate and kill people we view as enemies, they will become our enemies even if they were not enemies before we hated and killed them. People respond to how they are treated. It's like the dog at the state fair.

And yet the appeal of religion is at least partly the realization that we would all be a lot safer if the whole world loved each other, if we all acted as if we were of the same family, if we all helped the hungry to have enough to eat, if we cared for the sick, if we immersed all children in love, and if we loved not only our neighbors but also our enemies. We look with admiration at people like Desmond Tutu, Socrates, Gandhi, Abraham Lincoln, Buddha, Jesus, St. Francis, Mother Theresa, Elie Wiesel, and others whose lives of compassion, integrity, and courage have inspired countless others. They are role models *because their compassion went beyond their own tribe,* and their courage helped them take a stand for justice. Their lives went beyond and stood in direct opposition to a religion of *us against them.* They were able to reach the spark in the souls of others and help kindle a sacred fire, bringing light into the dark places of life.

Bishop Desmond Tutu is a role model who demonstrates that to love even our enemies can bring about a good result. If everyone were like him, Michael Hart would have listed Jesus as the world's most influential person instead of Muhammad.

I first heard him speak when I attended a meeting of the World Council of Churches in Vancouver British Columbia in July of 1983. I regret that I do not remember much of the content of his speech, but I remember crying while he spoke. His words of courage and compassion, of absolute conviction that Apartheid was wrong but with forgiveness toward those who were even at that time oppressing the black people of South Africa were stated in a way that conveyed a spirit of sorrow mixed with joy, of a conviction that the better angels of our nature could somehow overcome the evil which fostered oppression.

When the system of apartheid was dismantled, it was for the most part the result of two men: Nelson Mandela and Desmond Tutu. Desmond Tutu became chairman of the Truth and Reconciliation Committee in South Africa, and it was chiefly through his strength of personality that civil war was avoided between the majority black population and the white people who had formally oppressed them. He held fast to his conviction that revenge was not a good idea; that if a person confessed his crimes and indicated where the bodies could be found so that their families could properly bury and grieve for them, that person should be given amnesty.

The strength of his personality was the result of his strong faith in God. His book, *No Future Without Forgiveness,* is dedicated to the women and the "little people" of South Africa. He makes it clear in this book that his religious faith and his belief in the power of love and forgiveness gave him the courage to persevere until, as Anne Frank said in her diary, "things come out right."

His book *God Has a Dream* also offers an insight into the way he lives. He begins with a chapter called "God Believes in Us," and starts each chapter with these words: *Dear Child of God*. It is a book filled with hope.

*This is a **moral** universe, which means that, despite all the evidence that seems to be to the contrary, there is no way that evil and injustice and oppression and lies can have the last word. … God is in charge. That is what had upheld the morale of our people, to know that in the end good will prevail.*

Thanks to his leadership and the hope and faith South Africa emerged as a model for all people who have been divided into *us against them*. Bishop Tutu views all human beings as *us*. Even during Apartheid in South Africa he saw the white oppressors as brothers, as part of the same family of God. The struggle was not *us against them*. He says that peace came about due to the power of transfiguration:

The principle of transfiguration is at work when something so unlikely as the brown grass that covers our veld in winter becomes bright green again. Or when the tree with gnarled leafless branches bursts forth with the sap flowing so that the birds sit chirping in the leafy branches. Or when the once dry streams gurgle with swift-flowing water. When winter gives way to spring and nature seems to experience its own resurrection.

The principle of transfiguration says nothing, no one and no situation, is "untransfigurable," that the whole of creation, nature, waits expectantly for its transfiguration, when it will be released from its bondage and share in the glorious liberty of the children of God, when it will not be just dry inert matter but will be translucent with divine glory.

He has just published a new book called "Made for Goodness: And Why This Makes All the Difference." He wrote it with his daughter Mpho A. Tutu. It also is a book well worth reading and thinking about. His belief is that all human beings are created in the image of God and eventually, because that is our nature, goodness will eventually win out over hate and cruelty. I sure hope he is right.

Chapter Thirty Three
Bishop Shannon:
When the Cost of Being One of Us is Too Great

Nicole, I wish you could have met Bishop James P. Shannon, who I mentioned earlier. He is one of those people who somehow found a way to transcend the instinct for *self* preservation so that he could view all humans as *us*. Much of his life is recorded in his autobiography, a book titled *Reluctant Dissenter*. He was my mentor and my friend.

Earlier in this letter, which is now becoming a book, I told you how I met him. But I didn't really start to know him until I was a freshman at St. Thomas College, now St. Thomas University. At the opening convocation he talked about the Pony Express and an ad that ran in an 1860 California newspaper :

"Wanted. Young, skinny, wiry fellows not over 18. Must be expert riders, willing to risk death daily. Orphans preferred."

He talked about Bronco Charlie Miller who was only 11 years old when he began riding for the Pony Express, and Buffalo Bill Cody, the most famous rider. But most of all, he talked about the kind of person who would accept such a challenge. *Willing to risk death daily.* A person of courage and commitment. *Expert riders.* A person who has developed a skill. He suggested that each of us could be that kind of a person, that if we knew our lives would count; we would live to the fullest, dedicated to our country and to our God. That was the first time I *felt* and in some way knew that it would be possible for me to have a vision that involved being the best I could be.

There was something about the way he talked that inspired me, that made me feel that I could make a difference. Partly it had to do with what he said, but it had a lot to do with how he said it. It was like the challenge of President Kennedy when he urged us to ask not what our country could do for us, but what we could do for our country. It was like the dream that we could go to the moon, requiring not only engineers but those who would risk their lives as astronauts. We could do it; all we needed was the inspiration to believe that we could do it.

Each morning at about 7:00 Father Shannon would celebrate mass, and it was important for him to have an altar boy participate with him in the responses of the congregation. So I volunteered. Each weekday morning for the next three years I would arrive on campus at 6:45 and we, a congregation of two, would say mass.

Introibo ad altare Dei

I will approach the altar of God. That is how our day began, with the first words of the Latin mass. I would receive communion from him each day, or rather, most days. Some days I would not be able to arrive that early. Sometimes we would have a short time to just talk after mass, a way to get better acquainted and to develop a friendship. Following mass, I would go to class where the professor would lead us in a prayer of St. Thomas Aquinas:

Grant, O Merciful God, that I may ardently desire, prudently examine, truthfully acknowledge, and perfectly accomplish what is pleasing to Thee for the praise and glory of Thy holy name.

I am not sure that this prayer had any impact on me at the time. It was just part of a ritual that we went through at the beginning of each class period. But as I look back on it now, I realize that this prayer was meant to remind us of our relationship to God, and to indicate that what we were learning was significant, important enough to pray about. Prayer was clearly a crucial (from the Latin word *crux,* which also means "cross") part of Father Shannon's life, and as students of the college of which he was the president, he wanted it to be influential in our lives.

I followed his career with interest, and he followed mine. When I won the national essay contest about youth's role in foreign policy and got to meet President Kennedy at the Oval Office in the White House as well as our senators from Minnesota, he was as proud as anyone. And when the pope appointed him as a bishop during my last year at St.

Thomas, and I was at his installation service at the Cathedral in St. Paul, I was proud of him, of his integrity, his compassion, and his courage.

As a newly ordained priest, he had been appointed to help the bishop at the St. Paul Cathedral and was one morning called to respond to an emergency. The Minnesota Mining and Manufacturing plant in St. Paul was on fire and there had already been one explosion. Many people were killed; some were trapped in the rubble. They needed a priest to give comfort and last rites.

In his autobiography he describes what happened when he arrived:

The scene there was pandemonium. The explosion had wrecked the elevators and blown out the solid concrete stairways in the building. It was a bitterly cold day. ... Near the entrance to the shattered building a young, nervous fireman came over to me and said quietly that he was a Catholic and that he was new on the force. This was his first emergency. He was afraid to go into the building because the chief had told him that a second explosion was still expected, or at least possible, because of a ruptured gas line.

I tried to remind him of his special duties to serve the public, even at risk to himself. I said that he and I had to go where we were needed, not just where we were safe.

But just then the fire chief announced on a bullhorn that the building could totally collapse at any minute, so until further notice all firemen were forbidden to enter the building. However, he needed a Priest to enter with him to find the dying, to offer comfort. Father Shannon writes, "As I pulled on a hard hat and followed the chief into the building the young fireman patted me on the back." The scene he then describes reminds me of what witnesses and firefighters have said about the collapse of the Twin Towers on 9-11, except that it was sixteen degrees below zero and water from the fire hoses was ankle deep. He anointed over a dozen dying and dead people that day. He was a man of courage and compassion, a bishop who walked side-by-side, arm-in-arm with Dr. Martin Luther King Jr. at Selma Alabama, a leader who took a stand for what he thought was right.

I looked forward to reading the columns he wrote -- first in the Catholic newspaper, and then in the Minneapolis Star and Tribune. He opposed the Vietnam War when he realized how much it was costing -- the blood of over 50,000 Americans, the fragmentation of America with one group of people against another, tensions escalating so that the National Guard was called to quell a protest at Kent State, leading to the shooting and killing of some of the protesters. Freedom of Speech seemed eroded. So little visible payoff for so much sacrifice.

He was a man of courage and a person who used his voice, sometimes at great personal cost. He not only publically protested the war, but he stood up to the pope when he disagreed with the pope's encyclical that denied Catholic couples any form of birth control that went against "nature." Only abstinence or a "rhythm" method that sought to avoid sex during a time the woman might ovulate was permissible. His failure to give obedience to the pope cost him his position as bishop, but he kept his integrity. He was a great influence on me, and was a source of courage for me when I decided to marry Gail in the Lutheran Church.

I met with him in his office at St. Thomas during the fall of 1962. I told him I couldn't stay at a Catholic College, couldn't say mass with him any more, because my pastor, a priest, had told me and my family that I would be excommunicated by my decision to marry outside of the Catholic Church. I was no longer one of *us*.

He paused for a moment, and then told me that he knew something of Martin Luther. Of course I knew that, because his Ph.D. from Yale was in American History, but his interest was also in church history.

From what I remember," he said, "Martin Luther believed that a person needed more than anything to follow his own conscience, if it was informed by reason and Scripture. I have to say that I agree with him, and you have my blessing if that is what you are doing.

He came to talk to the students and faculty at St. Olaf College a few years later when I was teaching there, and I invited him to our home in Northfield, Minnesota. As we sat around our table he shared that when he had been appointed bishop, his took the motto: *mea omnia tua* for his coat of arms. "My all for you." These are the words used in the Bible by the father when the older brother of the prodigal son complains about the feast given for the returning son. The father says to the older son,

"All that I have is yours." *Mea Omnia Tua.* That is how Father Shannon, as he became Bishop Shannon, committed himself to Jesus. *Mea Omnia Tua.* For him Jesus came alive in the scriptures, and gave him the desire to follow as best he could the example set by Jesus. It was his faith in Jesus that allowed him to be the person who inspired me.

The last time I saw him was in the late 1990's. We met in his office at General Mills when he was in charge of the General Mills Foundation, helping decide who received grants. He was married then, and talked about how grateful he was to his wife Ruth for coming to him when many of his friends abandoned him, and more than once he indicated how much he loved her.

I mention James Shannon because he is an example for me of a person whose religious faith informed his life and inspired others, including me. He in turn, like many others, was inspired by the life and teachings of Christ and by people he admired. From Martin Luther to Martin Luther King Jr., from Paul of Tarsus to Mother Teresa, people whose lives have been inspired by their religious faith, people who have changed the world to be a more compassionate, loving place. Though history and our own lives contain many examples of people like Desmond Tutu and Bishop Shannon, sometimes it seems as if us against them and wars dominate the headlines.

But we have a choice.

And that leads to where we are now, wrestling with God because the Church often advocates *us against them*, and you have friends who are being discriminated against. When Bishop Shannon was in that situation, he spoke up, was excommunicated, and nevertheless stuck with the Church for the rest of his life. Martin Luther did the same thing. But some people leave.

For you, it depends on how you can live your best life. Right now you are a person who tends to live in truth, to confront those who are doing things that are not right. That is good. Can you do this and still be one of us in the Church? That is one option. The other is to leave and to continue to live your life in truth and love.

What you do is important. And now goes by very quickly. That's the next chapter.

Chapter Thirty Four
Chickens On The Highway

There is only so much time to do what we want to do in life. That's something that I didn't realize for a long time, and most young people don't think about it. It seems like there is forever, but yet life has a limit. Let me tell you the story.

I was driving North on I-5 on a sunny summer day when I looked at the truck that was passing me on the driver's side. It was a truck carrying hundreds of wire cages, and inside the cages were live chickens, about four to a cage. The wind was blowing their feathers because we were going about 60 miles an hour. But as the truck passed me, one chicken pulled up right next to me and looked at me, and we made eye contact for a few seconds. I don't know what the chicken thought, but my thoughts were that this chicken was about to die. He was likely headed for Colonel Sanders and would be somebody's lunch in a day or so. He was on the highway leading toward his death, but he probably didn't realize it.

But then it hit me: I was on the same highway.

Likely I would have a lot longer trip than that chicken, but we would eventually find, both of us, the end of the journey. And along the way, there were things I need to do. I wanted to find out what those things were.

Well, I have an idea now. Maybe not specifically, but at least generally. One thing I know for sure, without any doubt, is that my life has to be, to put it in a kind of corny way, "on the highway of love." Without love, it doesn't make any sense to me. That is why you are so important to me. You bring me love, we share love. You are part of the love that we share as family. Gail and Laurie and Mary and Julie and Justin and Aaron and Kyle are part of that love that we share with you.

And I am so blessed that I have been a pastor and have had the opportunity to be with people in very intimate ways, in counseling, in serious illness, in joy and in sorrow, in weddings and baptisms and worship services and parties and all kinds of ways that have linked us together. It is a great life, even despite the frustrations and sorrows that come along. I have hurt when I have seen the Church turn against other people, but I have been lifted up by the love that is there too. That has been the topic of this letter, and it is about over. Just one more thing, on the next page.

Chapter Thirty Five
"GoodBye"

So that's it. Those are my thoughts about our conversation. I've thought about it and written it all down, but I would love to get together as soon as we get back from Fallbrook so we can talk some more. If I send this in to a publisher, I would like to use what I have written, but if you wouldn't like me to use your name, or if Justin and Aaron and Kyle don't want me to use their names, I'll change things a bit.

Mostly the theme of this book has been that religion is very misunderstood by many people who lose the focus of love, the very focus that is the reason for religion. This has caused many people to give up the Church, the Bible, and religion. I've given you my thoughts to help you decide whether you will be one of these people.

Most of all I am writing to encourage you to think your own thoughts, to follow your heart (did you know that en courage ment comes from French words? *Coeur* is the French word for heart, *en* means in, and *ment* means thing. To encourage means to be in your heart, encouragement means a thing of the heart.) and to keep our conversation going. You are a great help to me. I'm looking forward to getting back and meeting at the restaurant, at your house, at our house, or anywhere. Meanwhile, "Good Bye!".

Love,
Grandpa

P.S. Nicole,
Here is an email I just received. It is an update about Keith Anderson. I sure hope it turns out better than this email suggests.

They found Keith Anderson's truck on a road outside of Darrington last Friday. From the way the rain fell off the truck and the depth of the marks the rain made they know the truck has been there for 17 days. The keys were locked inside. They searched with dogs on Saturday and Sunday and called off the search today. No sign of Keith.

P.P.S. Nicole, this has been an adventure, and I have gained a lot from thinking about these important things in our lives and writing them to you. I am definitely planning to have these things published, mostly because you and Julie and Gail have given such great input and are encouraging me to do that. So, Gail has an idea. Would you be willing to write a Foreword to the book? Or an Afterword, at the very end of the book? Let me know.

Afterword

By Nicole

April 10, 2010
Dear Grandpa,

You have been a huge inspiration to me my whole life. Every memory I have with you is full of happiness and very special to me. I look forward to spending all the time I can with you. You are my role model. Grandpa, you saved my life. Both through this past summer and traumatizing memories in the past, you have been my soul support. I know now that I would not be here today if it wasn't for you. Your love, support and encouragement brought me back to life. You were the medicine to my illness. I didn't realize this at the time, but I have come to realize this within the past year. You were the light in my darkest, hardest times. You were there to listen to me. You believed in me and it showed. This year has been tough for me as well, and once again, you are right by my side helping me out. You are a huge support in my life and you keep me going.

I really enjoy meeting up with you each week. I have learned so much from you, this year especially. Without thinking about censoring what I would say, we openly talked about our thoughts. I appreciate that you fully listened to me and took the time to think about our conversations. Generations are changing, but I feel like we are the same person, simply living in two different times. You look at every situation from every view point, and focus on loving everyone, not turning against them because they are "different." I wish every person in the world would understand this. I am so happy that you understand, especially since you are a pastor and you are extremely involved in your church. The fact that you are able to accept everyone and not judge or be closed minded says everything about you. You are amazing and you inspire me to love and do better for this world.

Your book puts into words the actions you show on a daily basis. I am so glad that others may now read what you have taught me my entire life. Your idea of "us against them" teaches to openly love everyone, putting aside all differences. Love is the key factor. You are love grandpa. You show love by example daily, preach it as a pastor, sing in the choir at your church, and have now written a book about it. I am so proud of you and I love your kind words and thoughtful actions. People who know you

157

understand how loving and nice you are, and the people who don't know you are lucky to read your thoughts and ideas. I love your book. It is easy to read, put together nicely and has great stories. The stories you tell relate to your message that love is the most important thing in the world. I wholly agree with you. Love is the most important thing. Without love, there is nothing but darkness, hard times, and emptiness. I completely agree and understand your statement that God *is* love. Love is powerful. God is powerful. Although you have taught me this my whole life, your book has strengthened my views on both God and love. You opened my eyes to love. I can feel it. I can see it.

I think it is so awesome how you tell the stories and talk about how important it is for us to remember who we are and who created us. It is crucial to know we are good. Everyone is good, and everyone should know that. It is easy for one to forget how good they are, so it is very important to love and let people know they are loved. You are a prime example of letting everyone know they are loved. You reminded me how good I am when I was lost and "dead." Love pulls people out of darkness whether they realize it or not. Thank you so much for teaching me that everyone is made in the image of their Savior. Honestly, it is the most important thing I have ever learned. Understanding that God is love has changed my life for the better.

Thank you so much for the wonderful book you have written. You have opened my eyes to creation, love, and acceptance. Without your wisdom and support, I would not be the person I am today. You have a strong, positive influence on me and I thank you so much for that. I love you and I am so happy for your constant presence in my life. Every time I am with you I feel comfortable and always leave feeling good about myself. It takes a unique individual to make such an impact on others, like you do for me. You are very special and I want you to know how much I appreciate your devotion and love for me. Your book is the most amazing thing that has ever happened to me. The fact you wrote this to me and expressed your feelings and thoughts and took the time to write this book touches me deeply. Thank you Grandpa, I love you chair.

Love,
Nicole

Bibliography

Anderson, Bernhard W. *Creation versus Chaos: Man's historic struggle for survival, seen through the reinterpretation of mythical symbolism in the Bible.* New York: Association Press, 1967.

Andrae, Tor. *Mohammed: The Man and His Faith.* Translated by Theophil Menzel. New York: Harper Torchbooks/The Cloister Library. Harper & Brothers, 1960.

Augustine. *The Confessions of St. Augustine.* Translated by R.S. Pine-Coffin. New York: Penguin, 1961

Bettelheim, Bruno. *The Uses of Enchantment: The Meaning and Importance of Fairy Tales.* New York: Alfred A. Knopf, 1976.
This book, along with Freud's *Interpretation of Dreams,* is suggestive of how to interpret symbols from the unconscious, including not only fairy tales and dreams, but also the symbols in legends, myths, and biblical stories. This book provides helpful material for the interpretation of the story of Adam and Eve.

The Oxford Annotated Bible, revised standard version, edited by Herbert G. May and Bruce M. Metzger. Oxford University Press, Inc., 1962.
All English Bibles are part translation and part interpretation of the Hebrew and Greek original, as is shown by the two translations of Eve's "curse" in Chapter Twelve of this book. The Oxford Annotated Bible is a reliable translation and usually indicates passages where various interpretations are possible.

Biblia Hebraica, secundum editions. Editio Sterotypa C. Tauchnith, Lipsiae, 1911.

Blehn, Eric. *The Only Thing Worth Dying For: How Eleven Green Berets Forged a New Afghanistan.* New York: Harper: An Imprint of HarperCollinsPublishers, 2010.

Bloom, Harold. *The Book of J Translated from the Hebrew by David Rosenberg.* New York: Vintage Books, a Division of Random House, Inc., 1991.

The translation of the story of Adam and Eve gives a vibrant understanding of the text, and the history of the part of the Bible written by "J" is very helpful. This is the most interesting translation of Genesis that I have encountered, and is especially helpful in interpreting the Hebrew symbols as well as words. It provides a corrective for the idea that women are cursed by God to be submissive to men.

Bongard, Jerry. *The Near-Birth Experience: A Journey to the Center of Self.* New York: Marlowe and Company, 2000.

This book presents evidence that the womb is indeed the Garden of Eden, and that under certain circumstances we can remember the safety, nurture, and even the presence of God with us before birth.

Borg, Marcus. *Meeting Jesus AGAIN for the First Time.* New York: HarperSanFrancisco, a division of HarperCollins, 1995.

_____. *Reading the Bible Again for the First Time: Taking the Bible seriously but not literally.* New York: HarperSanFrancisco, a division of HarperCollins, 2001.

_____. *The Heart of Christianity: Rediscovering a Life of Faith.* New York: HarperSanFrancisco, a division of HarperCollins, 2004.

These are just three of several helpful books written by Marcus Borg investigating what Jesus taught and how that can be compared to the orthodox doctrines, dogmas, and creeds of modern day Christianity. Marcus Borg is part of the "Jesus Seminar," investigating the various ways in which the biblical writers and other early scrolls and writings presented the religious beliefs of early Christianity. He suggests that the Bible is not to be always taken literally. See especially Chapter Four of *Reading the Bible Again* where he discusses the Adam and Eve story.

Browning, Christopher R. *Ordinary Men: Reserve Police Battalion 101 and the Final Solution in Poland.* New York: Aaron Asher Books, HarperPerennial, A Division of HarperCollinsPublishers, 1992.

This is a well researched insightful and wonderfully written report of the horrible and catastrophic events during World War II in which a police battalion carried out orders to kill Jews. It is a must read, indicating that people tend to go along with the group (*us*) even when the group decides to kill innocent people (*them.*).

Buber, Martin. *I And Thou* (2nd ed.) *trans. By Ronald Gregor Smith.* New York: Charles Scribner's Sons, 1958.

Campbell, Joseph. *Myths to Live by.* New York: Bantam Books, Inc., 1973.

_____. *The masks of God: Creative Mythology.* New York: The Viking Press, 1975. (Especially Chapters One and Three: Experience and Authority, and the Word behind Words.)

_____. *Primitive Mythology: The Masks of God.* New York: Penguin, 1976.

Campbell, Joseph and Moyers, B. *The Power of Myth.* (B.S. Flowers, Ed.). New York: Doubleday,
These four books explore the symbols of religious stories and myths, paving the way for a deeper meaning to creation stories that relate to our understanding of how we relate to the Creator and to Creation.

Carroll, James. *Constantine's Sword: The Church and the Jews.* New York: A Mariner Book, Houghton Mifflin Company, 2001.
This is a must-read detailed history of the relationship between Christians and the Jews throughout the 20 Centuries of Christianity, but especially since the time of Constantine. The chapters on Augustine and Constantine are especially relevant to this book, and the bibliography is excellent. Though a scholarly and well researched book, it also contains personal reflections taken from the experiences of the author.
Chamberlain, D.B. *Babies Remember Birth: And Other Extraordinary Scientific Discoveries about the Mind and Personality of Your Newborn.* Los Angeles: Tarcher, 1988.

Offers suggestive evidence that the womb and Eden have much in common, including not only nurture, but also awareness.

Childs, Brevard S. *Myth and Reality in the Old Testament, Second Edition*. London: SCM Press Ltd., 1962.
This book indirectly supports the womb as similar to Eden.

Chittister, Joan, OSB, *et al. The tent of Abraham: Stories of Hope and Peace for Jews, Christians, and Muslims*. Boston: Beacon Press, 2006.

Daly, Mary. *Beyond God the Father: Toward a Philosophy of Women's Liberation*. Boston, Beacon Press Books, 1985. (First published in 1973.)
Diamond, Jared. *Guns, Germs, and Steel: The Fates of Human Societies*. New York: W.W. Norton & Company, 1999.
A broad history of clashing societies, indicating reasons why one society prevails in its conflict with another. Especially interesting to me is the role played by germs. As a whole it supports the idea that human beings ordinarily find themselves in *us against them* relationships.

Eliade, Mircea. *Rites and Symbols of Initiation: The Mysteries of Birth and Rebirth, translated by Willard Trask*. Harper Torchbooks, Harper & Row, New York, 1975. First published in 1958 by Harper and Brothers under the title *Birth and Rebirth*. This book supports the idea that the symbolism of rites and rituals relate to passages of importance, such as birth and its need for a ritual such as baptism.

Feiler, Bruce. *Abraham: A Journey to the Heart of Three Faiths*. New York: Harper Perennial, 2005. The story of Abraham breaking the idol and blaming it on another idol comes from this book. It is also a good reference for the time of Abraham.

Feyerabend, Karl. *Langenscheidt pocket Hebrew dictionary to the Old Testament: Hebrew-English*. McGraw-Hill Book Company, Berlin, 1969. I used this mostly to check the translations of other authors.

Foss, Michael. *People of the First Crusade.* London: Caxton editions, an imprint of The Caxton Publishing Group, 2000.

This is a well written, well researched account of the first Crusade called by Pope Urban II in 1095, and is a very good introduction to Holy War.

Fox, Matthew. *Original Blessing: A Primer in Creation Spirituality* Santa Fe: Bear & Company, 1963.

Matthew Fox uses the term *Via Positiva* which is, as I understand it, a contrast to original sin. His emphasis is on the theme of the first story of creation, that everything God creates is good, and humans are very good. This book is filled with quotes from theologians and philosophers, but it is sometimes, for me, a little hard to follow.

Foxe, John. *Fox's Book of Martyrs, A History of the Lives, Sufferings, and Triumphant Deaths of the Primitive Protestant Martyrs from the Introduction of Christianity to the Latest Periods of Pagan, Popish, and Infidel Persecutions.* The John C. Winston Co., Chicago, Philadelphia, Toronto, 1926.

The first edition of this book was published in 1563 and had been republished many times since then. The 1563 edition contained 1800 pages. The 1570 edition contained 2300 pages. This book was republished by Xinware Corporation, Ottawa Canada in January of 2008.

Beginning with the death of the first Christian martyr, Stephen, this book lists details of the deaths of many hundreds of martyrs through Martin Luther. It is a horrendous example of the abuse of power, of the misuse of the Bible, and of the greed of those who killed others in order to possess their treasure, by using religion as their excuse to deal with the "threat" of heretics.

Frank, Anne. *The Diary of a Young Girl.* New York: Pocket Books, A Simon & Schuster division of Gulf and Western Corporation, 1953.

Fretheim, Terence E. *Creation, fall, and flood.* Minneapolis: Augsburg Publishing House, 1969.

Freud, Sigmund. *The Interpretation of Dreams. Translated from the German and edited by James Strachey.* New York: An Avon Library Book, 1966.

This is one of Freud's groundbreaking books indicating that the symbols of the unconscious mind are important messages. It helps pave the way for Jung and others who see the same kinds of messages in myths, fairy tales, parables and other stories as are found in dreams.

Gerbode, Frank A. *Beyond Psychology: An Introduction to Metapsychology, Third Edition.* Menlo Park: IRM Press, 1995.

Dr. Gerbode introduces new ways of viewing human behavior, and suggests an effective way of treating PTSD. It is from his book that the theory evolves of the four important events that impact our lives, and how important it is to view guilt as the result of unfulfilled intentions.

Gimbutas, Marija. *The Goddesses and Gods of Old Europe, 6500 – 3500 BC: Myths and Cult Images.* Berkeley and Los Angeles: University of California Press, 1982.

Filled with pictures and illustrations, this book presents convincing archeological evidence for Goddesses and Gods in the lands of the Bible before the time of Abraham.

Hafez, Mohammed M.: *Suicide Bombers in Iraq: The Strategy and Ideology of Martyrdom.* United States Institute of Peace Press, Washington D.C., 2007. See especially pp. 218-219.

A well-researched book with names and places of suicide bombings and the motivations for the bombers.

Hart, Michael H. *The 100: A Ranking of the Most Influential Persons in History.* New York: A Citadel Press Book, Published by Carol Publishing Group, 1994.

This is a thought-provoking suggestion regarding who contributed the most or had the most influence on human history.

Heine, Susanne. *Matriarchs, Goddesses, and Images of God: A Critique of a Feminist Theology.* Translated by John Bowden. Minneapolis: Augsburg Publishing House, 1989. (Original German edition published

1987 under the title *WIEDERBELEBUNG DER GOTTINNEN?*
Copyright Verlag Vandenhoeck & Ruprect, Gottingen. This book is
a critique of the evidence of matriarchal societies before the time of
Abraham.

Jampolsky, Gerald G., M.D. *Love is Letting God of Fear.* Berkeley:
Celestial Arts, 1979 and 2004.

Jewett, Paul. *Man as Male and Female.* Grand Rapids: William B.
Eerdmans Publishing Company, 1975.

Jung, C.G. *Psychology & Religion.* New Haven and London: Yale
University Press, 1938.

Kelsey, Morton T. *God, Dreams, and Revelation: A Christian
Interpretation of Dreams.* Augsburg Publishing House, Minneapolis,
1974. Though not directly, it indirectly gives support for the interpretation
of the story of Adam and Eve as being symbolic in the same way dreams
are symbolic.

*The Koran: Commonly called The Alcoran of Mohammed; Translated
into English immediately From the Original Arabic by George Sale, Gent.,
Fifth Edition.* Philadelphia: J.W. Moore, 1855. (This is an early edition
in English. Any version should suffice. Newer editions spell, in English,
the book as Qu'ran.)

Luther, Martin. *Luther's works, Vol. 1: Lectures on Genesis.* Edited by
Jaroslav Pelikan. Concordia Publishing House, St. Louis, 1958.
These writings show how Martin Luther understood the story of
Adam and Eve as a literal history of two people, and as an Augustinian
monk he supports the interpretation of Augustine that people are born
into a state of original sin.

Kung, Hans. *Christianity: Essence, History, and Future.* Translated
by John Bowden. New York: Continuum, 1995.

Luther's works, Vol. 1: Lectures on Genesis. Edited by Jaroslav Pelikan. Concordia Publishing House, St. Louis, 1958.

Malcomson, Scott L. *One Drop of Blood: The American Misadventure of Race.* New York: Farrar Straus Giroux, 2000.

Miller, Aaron David. *The Much Too Promised Land: America's Elusive Search for Arab-Israeli Peace.* New York: Bantam Books, 2008.

Morris, Joan. *The Lady was a Bishop: The hidden history of women with clerical ordination and the jurisdiction of bishops.* New York: The Macmillan Company, Collier-Macmillan Limited, London, 1973.

Needleman, Jacob. *The American Soul: Rediscovering the Wisdom of the Founders.* Jeremy P. Tarcher/Putnam, a Member of Penguin Group (USA) Inc., New York, 2002. This book contains a version of He Who Holds the Sky With Both Hands.

Neihardt, John G. *Black Elk Speaks: Being the Life Story of a Holy Man of the Oglala Sioux As Told through John G. Neihardt (Flaming Rainbow).* Lincoln and London: Bison Book, University of Nebraska Press, 1988. (Text is from the 1932 edition published by William Morrow and Co.)
This provides a version of history from the losing side, well written, as an example of *us against them.*

Netanyahu, B. *The Origins of the Inquisition in Fifteenth Century Spain.* New York: Random House, 1995.
A wonderfully researched and brilliantly written book indicating that the persecution of Jews came about in large measure because the majority populations considered them to be "other," and successful. The "otherness" increased when the Jews were labeled as a separate race. Mr. Netanyahu dedicates this book to the memory of his son Jonathan, who led the Israeli special forces in the raid on Entebbe to free hostages of Idi Amin. This dedication indicates a personal reason to investigate why not only the Spanish Inquisition but also other pogroms and the

Holocaust tended to target Jews as *them*. He says that it is part of our human nature to regard strangers with *xenophobia*.

Pagels, Elaine. *Adam, Eve, and the Serpent*. New York: Random House, 1988.
This book investigates the story of Adam and Eve and paves the way for an interpretation very different from the traditional one proposed by Augustine. Elaine Pagels is a scholar who is especially known for her research into the Gnostic gospels.

Ruether, Rosemary Radford. *Faith and Fratricide: The Theological Roots of Anti-Semitism*. New York: Seabury, 1974.

Salinger, J.D. *The Catcher in the Rye*. New York: A Bantam Book, published by arrangement with Little, Brown and Company, Inc., 1964.

Sanday, Peggy Reeves. *Female Power and Male Dominance: On the Origins of Sexual Inequalities*. Cambridge: Cambridge University Press, 1981.

Shannon, James Patrick. *Reluctant Dissenter: An Autobiography*. New York: A crossroad Book, The Crossroad Publishing Company, 1998.
Bishop Shannon writes of a first-hand conflict with a religion he loves, and he is an example of one who follows his conscience even though it means being excluded from the people who have been *us* and who then regard him as *them*.

Shlain, Leonard. *The Alphabet Versus the Goddess: The Conflict Between Word and Image*. New York: The Penguin Group, Penguin Putnam Inc., 1999.

Smith, Malcolm. *Thou Shalt Not Kill: Genocide in Central Africa*. LaVergne, TN: AuthorHouse, 2007.

A Catholic Priest experiences genocide happening in his parish in Burundi, Central Africa and details how it has affected his faith and life.

Stanton, Elizabeth Cady and the Revising Committee. *The Woman's Bible*. Coalition Task Force on Women and Religion, Seattle, 1974. (First published in 1898 by European Publishing Co., New York).

The comments on Genesis in *The Woman's* Bible are foundational for an understanding of the first two stories in the Bible, and the is one of the first important books to suggest that the story of Adam and Eve was written and put into the Bible to support the idea of man's dominance over women.

Stone, Merlin. *When God was a Woman*. New York: Barnes & Noble Books, 1976.

Taylor Jeremy. *Where People Fly and Water Runs Uphill: Using dreams to tap the wisdom of the unconscious*. New York: Warner Books, 1992.

An excellent reference regarding the symbolism of the unconscious, especially as used in dreams, but it is helpful in interpreting fairy tales and biblical stories that reach into the unconscious mind or the soul.

The Torah: The Five Books of Moses. A New Translation of The Holy Scriptures according to the traditional Hebrew text, Second Edition. Philadelphia: The Jewish Publication Society of America, 1982.

Tutu, Desmond Mpilo. *No Future Without Forgiveness*. New York: An Image Book, published by Doubleday, a division of Random House, Inc., 1999.

This is an excellent first-hand report of the Truth and Reconciliation Committee in South Africa, and it stresses the importance of forgiveness.

____. *God Has a Dream: A Vision of Hope for Our Time*.

This book stresses the relationship of all human s as children of God.

Tutu, Desmond M. and Mpho A. *Made For Goodness And Why This Makes All the Difference.* New York: HarperCollins e-books, 2010.

Tillich, Paul. *Systematic Theology, Vol. 2: Existence and the Christ.* New York: The University of Chicago Press, Harper and Row, 1967.
Tillich's theology of sin as alienation, and his suggestions about the story of Adam and Eve are important for a new understanding of that story and its relationship to baptism.

Van Vuuren, Nancy. *The subversion of women as practiced by Churches, witch-hunters and other sexists.* Philadelphia: The Westminster Press, 1973

Vivekananda, Swami. Edited by Advaita Ashrama. *Selections From The Complete Works of Swami Vivekananda.* Calcutta: Advaita Ashrama, 1991

Walker, Willison. *A History of the Christian Church.* New York: Charles Scribner's Sons, 1959.

Westermann, Claus. *The Genesis Accounts of Creation,* translated by Norman E. Wagner Facet Books, Philadelphia: Fortress Press, 1964.

Wiesel, Elie. *Legends of our time.* New York: Avon Books, 1968.

___. *The Night Trilogy: Night, Dawn, Day.* New York: Hill and Wang, 2008.
These two books are among many written by a winner of the Nobel Peace Prize, a survivor of Auschwitz and other camps during WWII. They are eloquent in their quest for God in the midst of the experience of being totally abandoned to the forces of evil.

Wilson, Marvin R. *Our Father Abraham: Jewish Roots of the Christian Faith.* Grand Rapids, Michigan: William B. Eerdmans Publishing Company and Center For Judaic-Christian Studies, Dayton, Ohio. 1989.

Zeitlin, Irving. *Jesus and the Judaism of His Time.* New York: Polity Press, 1988.

The quote used in the chapter on the crusades I found on the internet:

Kill Them All! God will know his own! (*Tuez-les tous; Dieu reconnaitra les siens.* Quoted from Tugwell, Simon. *Early Dominicans.* Paulist Press. ISBN 0-8091-2414-9. 1982, pp. 114-115; Retrieved from http://en.wikipedia.org/wiki/Arnaud_Amalric

CPSIA information can be obtained at www.ICGtesting.com
Printed in the USA
BVOW08s0025050214

343953BV00001B/50/P